The Burning Spear

*Being the Experiences of Mr. John Lavender in the
Time of War*

John Galsworthy

The Burning Spear
John Galsworthy

© 1st World Library – Literary Society, 2004
PO Box 2211
Fairfield, IA 52556
www.1stworldlibrary.org
First Edition

LCCN: 2004091228

Softcover ISBN: 1-59540-666-2
eBook ISBN: 1-59540-766-9

Purchase *"The Burning Spear"*
as a traditional bound book at:
www.1stWorldLibrary.org/purchase.asp?ISBN=1-59540-666-2

1st World Library Literary Society is a nonprofit organization dedicated to promoting literacy by:

- Creating a free internet library accessible from any computer worldwide.
- Hosting writing competitions and offering book publishing scholarships.

Readers interested in supporting literacy through sponsorship, donations or membership please contact:
literacy@1stworldlibrary.org
Check us out at: www.1stworldlibrary.org

The Burning Spear
contributed by the Mahaney Family
in support of
1st World Library Literary Society

NOTE: John Galsworthy said of this work: "'The Burning Spear' was revenge of the nerves. It was bad enough to have to bear the dreads and strains and griefs of war." Several years after its first publication he admitted authorship and it was included in the collected edition of his works. D.W.

> "With a heart of furious fancies,
> Whereof I am commander,
> With a burning spear and a horse of air
> In the wilderness I wander;
> With a night of ghosts and shadows
> I summoned am to tourney
> Ten leagues beyond the wide world's end
> For me it is no journey."
>
> TOM O'BEDLAM

I

THE HERO

In the year -- there dwelt on Hampstead Heath a small thin gentleman of fifty-eight, gentle disposition, and independent means, whose wits had become somewhat addled from reading the writings and speeches of public men. The castle which, like every Englishman, he inhabited was embedded in lilac bushes and laburnums, and was attached to another castle, embedded, in deference to our national dislike of uniformity, in acacias and laurustinus. Our gentleman, whose name was John Lavender, had until the days of the Great War passed one of those curious existences are sometimes to be met with, in doing harm to nobody. He had been brought up to the Bar, but like most barristers had never practised, and had spent his time among animals and the wisdom of the past. At the period in which this record opens he owned a young female sheep-dog called Blink, with beautiful eyes obscured by hair; and was attended to by a thin and energetic housekeeper, in his estimation above all weakness, whose name was Marian Petty, and by her husband, his chauffeur, whose name was Joe.

It was the ambition of our hero to be, like all public men, without fear and without reproach. He drank not, abstained from fleshly intercourse, and habitually spoke the truth. His face was thin, high cheek-boned, and not unpleasing, with one loose eyebrow over which he had no control; his eyes, bright and of hazel hue, looked his fellows in the face without seeing what was in it. Though his moustache was still dark, his thick waving hair was permanently white, for his study was lined from floor to ceiling with books, pamphlets, journals, and the recorded utterances of great mouths. He was of a frugal habit, ate what was put before him without question, and if asked what he would have, invariably answered: "What is there?" without listening to the reply. For at mealtimes it was his custom to read the writings of great men.

"Joe," he would say to his chauffeur, who had a slight limp, a green wandering eye, and a red face, with a rather curved and rather redder nose, "You must read this."

And Joe would answer:

"Which one is that, sir?"

"Hummingtop; a great man, I think, Joe."

"A brainy chap, right enough, sir."

"He has done wonders for the country. Listen to this." And Mr. Lavender would read as follows: "If I had fifty sons I would give them all. "If I had forty daughters they should nurse and scrub and weed and fill shells; if I had thirty country-houses they should all be hospitals; if I had twenty pens I would use them all day long; if had ten voices they should never cease to inspire and aid my country."

"If 'e had nine lives," interrupted Joe, with a certain suddenness, "'e'd save the lot."

Mr. Lavender lowered the paper.

"I cannot bear cynicism, Joe; there is no quality so unbecoming to a gentleman."

"Me and 'im don't put in for that, sir."

"Joe, Mr. Lavender would say you are, incorrigible...."

Our gentleman, in common with all worthy of the name, had a bank-book, which, in hopes that it would disclose an unsuspected balance, he would have "made up" every time he read an utterance exhorting people to invest and save their country.

One morning at the end of May, finding there was none, he called in his housekeeper and said:

"Mrs. Petty, we are spending too much; we have again been exhorted to save. Listen! 'Every penny diverted from prosecution of the war is one more spent in the interests of the enemies of mankind. No patriotic person, I am confident; will spend upon him or herself a stiver which could be devoted to the noble ends so near to all our hearts. Let us make every spare copper into bullets to strengthen the sinews of war!' A great speech. What can we do without?"

"The newspapers, sir."

"Don't be foolish, Mrs. Petty. From what else could we draw our inspiration and comfort in these terrible days?"

Mrs. Petty sniffed. "Well, you can't eat less than you do," she said; "but you might stop feedin' Blink out of your rations - that I do think."

"I have not found that forbidden as yet in any public utterance," returned Mr. Lavender; "but when the Earl of Betternot tells us to stop, I shall follow his example, you may depend on that. The country comes before everything. "Mrs. Petty tossed her head and murmured darkly

"Do you suppose he's got an example, Sir?"

"Mrs. Petty," replied Mr. Lavender, "that is quite unworthy of you. But, tell me, what can we do without?"

"I could do without Joe," responded Mrs. Petty, "now that you're not using him as chauffeur."

"Please be serious. Joe is an institution; besides, I am thinking of offering myself to the Government as a speaker now that we may use gas."

Ah!" said Mrs. Petty.

"I am going down about it to-morrow."

"Indeed, sir!"

"I feel my energies are not fully employed."

"No, sir?"

"By the way, there was a wonderful leader on potatoes yesterday. We must dig up the garden. Do you know what the subsoil is?"

"Brickbats and dead cats, I expect, sir."

"Ah! We shall soon improve that. Every inch of land reclaimed is a nail in the coffin of our common enemies."

And going over to a bookcase, Mr. Lavender took out the third from the top of a pile of newspapers. "Listen!" he said. "'The problem before us is the extraction of every potential ounce of food. No half measures must content us. Potatoes! Potatoes! No matter how, where, when the prime national necessity is now the growth of potatoes. All Britons should join in raising a plant which may be our very salvation.

"Fudge!" murmured Mrs. Petty.

Mr. Lavender read on, and his eyes glowed.

"Ah!" he thought, "I, too, can do my bit to save England.... It needs but the spark to burn away the dross of this terrible horse-sense which keeps the country back.

"Mrs. Petty!" But Mrs. Petty was already not.

. . . .

The grass never grew under the feet of Mr. Lavender, No sooner had he formed his sudden resolve than he wrote to what he conceived to be the proper quarter, and receiving no reply, went down to the centre of the official world. It was at time of change and no small national excitement; brooms were sweeping clean, and new offices had arisen everywhere. Mr. Lavender passed bewildered among large stone buildings and small wooden buildings, not knowing where to go. He had bought no clothes since the beginning of the war, except the various Volunteer uniforms which the exigencies of a shifting situation had forced the authorities to withdraw from time to time; and his small shrunken figure struck somewhat vividly on the eye, with elbows and knees shining in the summer sunlight. Stopping at last before the only object which seemed unchanged, he said:

"Can you tell me where the Ministry is?"

The officer looked down at him.

"What for?"

"For speaking about the country."

"Ministry of Propagation? First on the right, second door on the left."

"Thank you. The Police are wonderful."

"None of that," said the officer coldly.

"I only said you were wonderful."

"I 'eard you."

"But you are. I don't know what the country would do without you. Your solid qualities, your imperturbable bonhomie, your truly British tenderness towards -- "

"Pass away!" said the officer.

"I am only repeating what we all say of you," rejoined Mr. Lavender reproachfully.

"Did you 'ear me say 'Move on,'" said the officer; "or must I make you an example?"

"YOU are the example," said Mr. Lavender warmly.

"Any more names," returned the officer, "and I take you to the station." And he moved out into the traffic. Puzzled by his unfriendliness Mr. Lavender resumed his search, and, arriving at the door indicated, went in. A dark, dusty, deserted corridor led him nowhere, till he came on a little girl in a brown frock, with her hair down her back.

"Can you tell me, little one -- " he said, laying his hand on her head.

"Chuck it!" said the little girl.

"No, no!" responded Mr. Lavender, deeply hurt. "Can you tell me where I can find the Minister?"

"'Ave you an appointment?

"No; but I wrote to him. He should expect me."

"Wot nyme?"

"John Lavender. Here is my card."

"I'll tyke it in. Wyte 'ere!"

"Wonderful!" mused Mr. Lavender; "the patriotic impulse already stirring in these little hearts! What was the stanza of that patriotic poet?

> "'Lives not a babe who shall not feel the pulse
> Of Britain's need beat wild in Britain's wrist.
> And, sacrificial, in the world's convulse
> Put up its lips to be by Britain kissed.'

"So young to bring their lives to the service of the country!"

"Come on," said the little girl, reappearing suddenly; "e'll see you."

Mr. Lavender entered a room which had a considerable resemblance to the office of a lawyer save for the absence of tomes. It seemed furnished almost exclusively by the Minister, who sat with knees crossed, in a pair of large round tortoiseshell spectacles, which did not, however, veil the keenness of his eyes. He was a man with close cropped grey hair, a broad, yellow, clean-shaven face, and thrusting grey eyes.

"Mr. Lavender," he said, in a raw, forcible voice; "sit down, will you?"

"I wrote to you," began our hero, "expressing the wish to offer myself as a speaker."

"Ah!" said the Minister. "Let's see - Lavender, Lavender. Here's your letter." And extracting a letter from a file he read it, avoiding with difficulty his tortoiseshell spectacles. "You want to stump the country? M.A., Barrister, and Fellow of the Zoological. Are you a good speaker?"

"If zeal --" began Mr. Lavender.

"That's it; spark! We're out to win this war, sir."

"Quite so," began Mr. Lavender. "If devotion -- "

"You'll have to use gas," said the Minister; and we don't pay."

"Pay!" cried Mr. Lavender with horror; "no, indeed!"

The Minister bent on him a shrewd glance.

"What's your line? Anything particular, or just general patriotism? I recommend that; but you'll have to put some punch into it, you know."

"I have studied all the great orators of the war, sir," said Mr. Lavender, "and am familiar with all the great writers on, it. I should form myself on them; and if enthusiasm -- "

"Quite!" said the Minister. "If you want any atrocities we can give you them. No facts and no figures; just general pat."

"I shall endeavour -- " began Mr. Lavender.

"Well, good-bye," said the Minister, rising. "When do you start?"

Mr. Lavender rose too. "To-morrow," he said, "if I can get inflated."

The Minister rang a bell.

"You're on your own, mind," he said. "No facts; what they want is ginger. Yes, Mr. Japes?"

And seeing that the Minister was looking over his tortoiseshell. spectacles at somebody behind him, Mr. Lavender turned and went out. In the corridor he thought, "What terseness! How different from the days when Dickens wrote his 'Circumlocution Office'! Punch!" And opening the wrong door, he found himself in the presence of six little girls in brown frocks, sitting against the walls with their thumbs in their mouths.

"Oh!" he said, "I'm afraid I've lost my way."

The eldest of the little girls withdrew a thumb.

"What d'yer want?"

"The door," said Mr. Lavender.

"Second on the right."

"Goodbye," said Mr. Lavender.

The little girls did not answer. And he went out thinking, "These children are really wonderful! What devotion one sees! And yet the country is not yet fully roused!"

II

THE VALET

Joe Petty stood contemplating the car which, purchased some fifteen years before had not been used since the war began. Birds had nested in its hair. It smelled of mould inside; it creaked from rust. "The Guv'nor must be cracked," he thought, "to think we can get anywhere in this old geyser. Well, well, it's summer; if we break down it won't break my 'eart. Government job - better than diggin' or drillin'. Good old Guv!" So musing, he lit his pipe and examined the recesses beneath the driver's seat. "A bottle or three," he thought, "in case our patriotism should get us stuck a bit off the beaten; a loaf or two, some 'oney in a pot, and a good old 'am.

"A life on the rollin' road -- ' 'Ow they can give 'im the job I can't think!" His soliloquy was here interrupted by the approach of his wife, bearing a valise.

"Don't you wish you was comin', old girl?" he remarked to her lightly.

"I do not; I'm glad to be shut of you. Keep his feet dry. What have you got under there?"

Joe Petty winked.

"What a lumbering great thing it looks!" said Mrs. Petty, gazing upwards.

"Ah!" returned her husband thoughtfully, we'll 'ave the population round us without advertisement. And taking the heads of two small boys who had come up, he knocked them together in an absent-minded fashion.

"Well," said Mrs. Petty, "I can't waste time. Here's his extra set of teeth. Don't lose them. Have you got your own toothbrush? Use it, and behave yourself. Let me have a line. And don't let him get excited." She tapped her forehead.

"Go away, you boys; shoo!"

The boys, now six in number, raised a slight cheer ; for at that moment Mr. Lavender, in a broad-brimmed grey felt hat and a holland dust-coat, came out through his garden-gate carrying a pile of newspapers and pamphlets so large that his feet, legs, and hat alone were visible.

"Open the door, Joe!" he said, and stumbled into the body of the vehicle. A shrill cheer rose from the eight boys, who could see him through the further window. Taking this for an augury Of success, Mr. Lavender removed his hat, and putting his head through the window, thus addressed the ten boys:

"I thank you. The occasion is one which I shall ever remember. The Government has charged me with the great task of rousing our country in days which demand of each of us the utmost exertions. I am proud to feel that I have here, on the very threshold of my task, an audience of bright young spirits, each one of whom in this democratic country has in him perhaps the makings of a General or even of a Prime Minister. Let it be your earnest endeavour, boys -- "

At this moment a piece of indiarubber rebounded from Mr. Lavender's forehead, and he recoiled into the body of the car.

"Are you right, sir?" said Joe, looking in; and without waiting for reply he started the engine. The car moved out amid a volley of stones, balls, cheers, and other missiles from the fifteen boys who pursued it with frenzy. Swaying slightly from side to side, with billowing bag, it gathered speed, and, turning a corner, took road for the country. Mr. Lavender, somewhat dazed, for the indiarubber had been hard, sat gazing through the little back window at the great city he was leaving. His lips moved, expressing unconsciously the sentiments of innumerable Lord Mayors: "Greatest City in the world, Queen of Commerce, whose full heart I can still hear beating behind me, in mingled pride and regret I leave you. With the most sacred gratitude I lay down my office. I go to other work, whose -- Joe!"

"Sir?"

"Do you see that?"

"I see your 'ead, that's all, sir."

"We seem to be followed by a little column of dust, which keeps ever at the same distance in the middle of the road. Do you think it can be an augury."

"No; I should think it's a dog."

"In that case, hold hard!" said Mr. Lavender, who had a weakness for dog's. Joe slackened the car's pace, and leaned his head round the comer. The column of dust approached rapidly.

"It is a dog," said Mr. Lavender, "it's Blink."

The female sheep-dog, almost flat with the ground from speed, emerged from the dust, wild with hair and anxiety, white on the cheeks and chest and top of the head, and grey in the body and the very little tail, and passed them like a streak of lightning.

"Get on!" cried Mr. Lavender, excited; "follow her she's trying to catch us up!"

Joe urged on the car, which responded gallantly, swaying from side to side, while the gas-bag bellied and shook; but the faster it went the faster the sheep-dog flew in front of it.

"This is dreadful!" said Mr. Lavender in anguish, leaning far out. "Blink! Blink!"

His cries were drowned in the roar of the car.

"Damn the brute!" muttered Joe at this rate she'll be over the edge in 'alf a mo'. Wherever does she think we are?"

"Blink! Blink!" wailed Mr. Lavender. "Get on, Joe, get on! She's gaining on us!"

"Well I never see anything like this," said Joe, "chasin' wot's chasing you! Hi! Hi!"

John Glasworthy

Urged on by their shouts and the noise of the pursuing car, the poor dog redoubled her efforts to rejoin her master, and Mr. Lavender, Joe, and the car, which had begun to emit the most lamentable creaks and odours, redoubled theirs.

"I shall bust her up," said Joe.

"I care not!" cried Mr. Lavender. "I must recover the dog."

They flashed through the outskirts of the Garden City. "Stop her, stop her!" called Mr. Lavender to such of the astonished inhabitants as they had already left behind. "This is a nightmare, Joe!"

"'It's a blinkin' day-dream," returned Joe, forcing the car to an expiring spurt.

"If she gets to that 'ill before we ketch 'er, we're done; the old geyser can't 'alf crawl up 'ills."

"We're gaining," shrieked Mr. Lavender; "I can see her tongue."

As though it heard his voice, the car leaped forward and stopped with a sudden and most formidable jerk; the door burst open, and Mr. Lavender fell out upon his sheep-dog.

Fortunately they were in the only bed of nettles in that part of the world, and its softness and that of Blink assuaged the severity of his fall, yet it was some minutes before he regained the full measure of his faculties. He came to himself sitting on a milestone, with his dog on her hind legs between his knees, licking his face clean, and panting down his throat.

"Joe," he said; "where are you"?

The voice of Joe replied from underneath the car: "Here sir. She's popped."

"Do you mean that our journey is arrested?"

"Ah! We're in irons. You may as well walk 'ome, sir. It ain't two miles.

"No! no!" said Mr. Lavender. "We passed the Garden City a little way back; I could go and hold a meeting. How long will you be?"

"A day or two," said Joe.

Mr. Lavender sighed, and at this manifestation of his grief his sheep-dog redoubled her efforts to comfort him. "Nothing becomes one more than the practice of philosophy," he thought. "I always admired those great public men who in moments of national peril can still dine with a good appetite. We will sit in the car a little, for I have rather a pain, and think over a speech." So musing he mounted the car, followed by his dog, and sat down in considerable discomfort.

"What subject can I choose for a Garden City?" he thought, and remembering that he had with him the speech of a bishop on the subject of babies, he dived into his bundle of literature, and extracting a pamphlet began to con its periods. A sharp blow from a hammer on the bottom of the car just below where Blink was sitting caused him to pause and the dog to rise and examine her tiny tail.

"Curious," thought Mr. Lavender dreamily, "how Joe always does the right thing in the wrong place. He is very English." The hammering continued, and the dog, who traced it to the omnipotence of her master, got up on the seat where she could lick his face. Mr. Lavender was compelled to stop.

"Joe," he said, leaning out and down; "must you?"

The face of Joe, very red, leaned out and up. "What's the matter now, sir?"

"I am preparing a speech; must you hammer?"

"No," returned Joe, "I needn't."

"I don't wish you to waste your time," said Mr Lavender.

"Don't worry about that, sir," replied Joe; "there's plenty to do."

"In that case I shall be glad to finish my speech."

Mr. Lavender resumed his seat and Blink her position on the floor, with her head on his feet. The sound of his voice soon rose again in the car like the buzzing of large flies. "'If we are to win this war we must have an ever-increasing population. In town and countryside, in the palace and the slum, above all in the Garden City, we must have babies.'"

Here Blink, who had been regarding him with lustrous eyes, leaped on to his knees and licked his mouth. Again Mr. Lavender was compelled to stop.

"Down, Blink, down! I am not speaking to you. 'The future of our country depends on the little citizens born now. I especially appeal to women. It is to them we must look -- '"

"Will you 'ave a glass, sir?"

Mr. Lavender saw before him a tumbler containing a yellow fluid.

"Joe," he said sadly, "you know my rule -- "

"'Ere's the exception, sir."

Mr. Lavender sighed. "No, no; I must practise what I preach. I shall soon be rousing the people on the liquor question, too."

Well, 'ere's luck," said Joe, draining the glass. "Will you 'ave a slice of 'am?"

"That would not be amiss," said Mr. Lavender, taking Joe's knife with the slice of ham upon its point. "'It is to them that we must look,'" he resumed, "'to rejuvenate the Empire and make good the losses in the firing-line.'" And he raised the knife to his mouth. No result followed, while Blink wriggled on her base and licked her lips.

"Blink!" said Mr. Lavender reproachfully. "Joe!"

"Sir!"

"When you've finished your lunch and repaired the car you will find me in the Town Hall or market-place. Take care of Blink. I'll tie her up. Have you some string?"

Having secured his dog to the handle of the door and disregarded the intensity of her gaze, Mr. Lavender walked back towards the Garden City with a pamphlet in one hand and a crutch-handled stick in the other. Restoring the ham to its nest behind his feet, Joe finished the bottle of Bass. "This is a bit of all right!" he thought dreamily. "Lie down, you bitch! Quiet! How can I get my nap while you make that row? Lie down! That's better."

Blink was silent, gnawing at her string. The smile deepened on Joe's face, his head fell a little one side his mouth fell open a fly flew into it.

"Ah!" he thought, spitting it out; "dog's quiet now." He slept.

III

MR. LAVENDER ADDRESSES A CROWD OF HUNS

"'Give them ginger!'" thought Mr. Lavender, approaching the first houses. "My first task, however, will be to collect them."

"Can you tell me," he said to a dustman, "where the market-place is?"

"Ain't none."

"The Town Hall, then?"

"Likewise."

"What place is there, then," said Mr. Lavender," where people congregate?"

"They don't."

"Do they never hold public meetings here?"

"Ah!" said the dustman mysteriously.

"I wish to address them on the subject of babies."

"Bill! Gent abaht babies. Where'd he better go?"

The man addressed, however, who carried a bag of tools, did not stop.

"You,'ear?" said the dustman, and urging his horse, passed on.

"How rude!" thought Mr. Lavender. Something cold and wet was pressed against his hand, he felt a turmoil, and saw Blink moving round and round him, curved like a horseshoe, with a bit of string dangling from her white neck. At that moment of discouragement the sight of one who believed in him gave Mr. Lavender nothing but pleasure. "How wonderful dogs are!" he murmured. The sheep-dog responded by bounds and ear-splitting barks, so that two boys and a little girl wheeling a perambulator stopped to look and listen.

"She is like Mercury," thought Mr. Lavender; and taking advantage of her interest in his hat, which she had knocked off in her effusions, he placed his hand on her head and crumpled her ear. The dog passed into an hypnotic trance, broken by soft grumblings of pleasure. "The most beautiful eyes in the world!" thought Mr. Lavender, replacing his hat; "the innocence and goodness of her face are entrancing."

In his long holland coat, with his wide-brimmed felt hat all dusty, and the crutch-handled stick in his hand, he had already arrested the attention of five boys, the little girl with the perambulator, a postman, a maid-servant, and three old ladies.

"What a beautiful dog yours is!" said one of the old ladies; "dear creature! Are you a shepherd?"

Mr. Lavender removed his hat.

"No, madam," he said; "a public speaker."

"How foolish of me!" replied the old lady.

"Not at all, madam; the folly is mine." And Mr. Lavender bowed. "I have come here to give an address on babies."

The old lady looked at him shrewdly, and, saying something in a low voice to her companions, passed on, to halt again a little way off.

In the meantime the rumour that there was a horse down in the Clemenceau Road had spread rapidly, and more boys, several little girls, and three soldiers in blue, with red ties, had joined the group round Mr. Lavender, to whom there seemed something more than providential in this rapid assemblage. Looking round him for a platform from which to address them, he saw nothing but the low wall of the little villa garden outside which he was standing. Mounting on this, therefore, and firmly grasping the branch of a young acacia tree to steady himself, he stood upright, while Blink, on her hind legs, scratched at the wall, whining and sniffing his feet.

Encouraged by the low murmur of astonishment, which swelled idly into a shrill cheer, Mr. Lavender removed his hat, and spoke as follows:

"Fellow Britons, at this crisis in the history of our country I make no apology for addressing myself to the gathering I see around me. Here, in the cradle of patriotism and the very heart of Movements, I may safely assume that you are aware of the importance of Man-power. At a moment when every man of a certain age and over is wanted at the front, and every woman of marrigeable years is needed in hospitals, in factories, on the land, or where not, we see as never before the paramount necessity of mobilizing the forces racial progress and increasing the numbers of our population. Not a man, not a woman can be spared from the great task in which they are now engaged, of defeating the common enemy. Side by side with our American cousins, with la belle France, and the Queen of the Adriatic, we are fighting to avert the greatest menace which ever threatened civilization. Our cruel enemies are strong and ruthless. While I have any say in this matter, no man or woman shall be withdrawn from the sacred cause of victory; better they should die to the last unit than that we should take our hands from the plough. But, ladies and gentlemen, we must never forget that in the place of every one who dies we must put two. Do not be content with ordinary measures; these are no piping times of peace. Never was there in the history of this country such a crying need for - for twins, if I may put it picturesquely. In each family, in each home where there are no families, let there be two babies where there was one, for thus only can we triumph over the devastation of this war." At this moment the now considerable audience, which had hitherto been silent, broke into a shrill "'Ear, 'ear!" and Mr. Lavender, taking his hand from the acacia branch to silence them, fell off the wall into the garden. Seeing her master thus vanish, Blink, who had never ceased to whine and sniff his toes, leaped over and landed on his chest. Rising with difficulty, Mr. Lavender found himself in front of an elderly man with a commercial cast of countenance, who said: "You're trespassing!"

"I am aware of it," returned Mr. Lavender and I beg your pardon. It was quite inadvertent, however.

"Rubbish!" said the man.

"I fell off the wall."

"Whose wall do you think it is?" said the man.

"How should I know?" said Mr. Lavender; "I am a stranger."

"Out you go," said the man, applying his boot to Blink.

"Mr. Lavender's eyes blazed." You may insult me," he said, "but you must not kick my dog, or I shall do you an injury.

"Try!" said the man.

"I will," responded Mr. Lavender, taking off his holland coat.

To what extremities he would have proceeded cannot be told, for at this moment the old lady who had taken him for a shepherd appeared on the path, tapping her forehead with finger.

"All right!" said the owner of the garden, "take him away."

The old lady laced her hand within Mr. Lavender's arm. "Come with me, sir," she said, "and your nice doggie."

Mr. Lavender, whose politeness to ladies was

invariable, bowed, and resuming his coat accompanied her through the 'garden gate. "He kicked my dog," he said; "no action could be more despicable."

"Yes, yes," said the old lady soothingly. "Poor doggie!"

The crowd, who had hoped for better things, here gave vent to a prolonged jeer.

"Stop!" said Mr. Lavender; "I am going to take a collection."

"There, there!" said the old lady. "Poor man!"

"I don't know what you mean by that, madam, said Mr. Lavender, whose spirit was roused; "I shall certainly take a collection, in the interests of our population. "So saying he removed his hat, and disengaging his arm from the old lady's hand, moved out into the throng, extending the hat. A boy took it from him at once, and placing it on his head, ran off, pursued by Blink, who, by barking and jumping up increased the boy's speed to one of which he could never have thought himself capable. Mr. Lavender followed, calling out "Blink!" at the top of his voice. The crowd followed Mr. Lavender, and the old lady followed crowd. Thus they proceeded until the boy, arriving at a small piece of communal water, flung the hat into the middle of it, and, scaling the wall, made a strategic detour and became a disinterested spectator among the crowd. The hat, after skimming the surface of the pond, settled like a water-lily, crown downwards, while Blink, perceiving in all this the hand of her master, stood barking at it wildly. Mr. Lavender arrived at the edge of the pond slightly in advance of the crowd.

"Good Blink!" he said. "Fetch it! Good Blink!"

Blink looked up into his face, and, with the acumen for which her breed is noted, perceiving he desired her to enter the water backed away from it.

"She is not a water dog," explained Mr. Lavender to the three soldiers in blue clothes.

"Good dog; fetch it!" Blink backed into the soldiers, who, bending down, took her by head tail, threw her into the pond, and encouraged her on with small stones pitched at the hat. Having taken the plunge, the intelligent animal waded boldly to the hat, and endeavoured by barking and making little rushes at it with her nose, to induce it to return to shore.

"She thinks it's a sheep," said Mr. Lavender; "a striking instance of hereditary instinct."

Blink, unable to persuade the hat, mounted it with her fore-paws and trod it under.

"Ooray!" shouted the crowd.

"Give us a shilling, guv'nor, an' I'll get it for yer?"

"Thank you, my boy," said Mr. Lavender, producing a shilling.

The boy - the same boy who had thrown it in - stepped into the water and waded towards the hat. But as he approached, Blink interposed between him and the hat, growling and showing her teeth.

"Does she bite?" yelled the boy.

"Only strangers," cried Mr. Lavender.

Excited by her master's appeal, Blink seized the jacket of the boy, who made for the shore, while the hat rested in the centre of the pond, the cynosure of the stones with which the soldiers were endeavouring to drive it towards the bank. By this, time the old lady had rejoined Mr. Lavender.

"Your nice hat she murmured.

"I thank you for your sympathy, madam," Lavender, running his hand through his hair; "in moments like these one realizes the deep humanity of the British people. I really believe that in no other race could you find such universal interest and anxiety to recover a hat. Say what you will, we are a great nation, who only, need rousing to show our best qualities. Do you remember the words of the editor: 'In the spavined and spatch-cocked ruin to which our inhuman enemies have reduced civilization, we of the island shine with undimmed effulgence in all those qualities which mark man out from the ravening beast'?"

"But how are you going to get your hat?" asked the old lady.

"I know not," returned Mr. Lavender, still under the influence of the sentiment he had quoted; "but if I had fifteen hats I would take them all off to the virtues which have been ascribed to the British people by all those great men who have written and spoken since the war began."

"Yes," said the old lady soothingly. "But, I think you had better come under my sunshade. The sun is very strong."

"Madam," said Mr. Lavender, "you are very good, but your sunshade is too small. To deprive you of even an inch of its shade would be unworthy of anyone in public life." So saying, he recoiled from the proffered sunshade into the pond, which he had forgotten was behind him.

"Oh, dear!" said the old lady; "now you've got your feet wet!"

"It is nothing," responded Mr. Lavender gallantly. And seeing that he was already wet, he rolled up his trousers, and holding up the tails of his holland coat, turned round and proceeded towards his hat, to the frantic delight of the crowd.

"The war is a lesson to us to make little of little things," he thought, securing the hat and wringing it out. "My feet are wet, but - how much wetter they would be in the trenches, if feet can be wetter than wet through," he mused with some exactitude. "Down, Blink, down!" For Blink was plastering him with the water-marks of joy and anxiety. "Nothing is quite so beautiful as the devotion of one's own dog," thought Mr. Lavender, resuming the hat, and returning towards the shore. The by-now-considerable throng were watching him with every mark of acute enjoyment; and the moment appeared to Mr. Lavender auspicious for addressing them. Without, therefore, emerging from the pond, which he took for his, platform, he spoke as follows:

"Circumstances over which I have no control have given me the advantage of your presence in numbers which do credit to the heart of the nation to which we all belong. In the midst of the greatest war which ever threatened the principle of Liberty, I rejoice to see so many people able to follow the free and spontaneous impulses of their inmost beings. For, while we must remember that our every hour is at the disposal of our country, we must not forget the maxim of our fathers: 'Britons never will be slaves.' Only by preserving the freedom of individual conscience, and at the same time surrendering it whole-heartedly to every which the State makes on us, can we hope defeat the machinations of the arch enemies of mankind."

At this moment a little stone hit him sharply on the hand.

"Who threw that stone?" said Mr. Lavender. "Let him stand out."

The culprit, no other indeed than he who had thrown the hat in, and not fetched it out for a shilling, thus menaced with discovery made use of a masterly device, and called out loudly:

"Pro-German!"

Such was the instinctive patriotism of the crowd that the cry was taken up in several quarters; and for the moment Mr. Lavender remained speechless from astonishment. The cries of "Pro-German!" increased in volume, and a stone hitting her on the nose caused Blink to utter a yelp; Mr. Lavender's eyes blazed.

"Huns!" he cried; "Huns! I am coming out."

With this prodigious threat he emerged from the pond

at the very moment that a car scattered the throng, and a well-known voice said:

"Well, sir, you 'ave been goin' it!"

"Joe," said Mr. Lavender, "don't speak to me!"

"Get in."

"Never!"

"Pro-Germans!" yelled the crowd.

"Get in!" repeated Joe.

And seizing Mr. Lavender as if collaring him at football, he knocked off his hat, propelled him into the car, banged the door, mounted, and started at full speed, with Blink leaping and barking in front of them.

Debouching from Piave Parade into Bottomley Lane he drove up it till the crowd was but a memory before he stopped to examine the condition his master. Mr. Lavender was hanging out of window, looking back, and shivering violently.

"Well, sir," said Joe. "I don't think!"

"Joe," said Mr. Lavender that crowd ought not to be at large. They were manifestly Huns.

"The speakin's been a bit too much for you, sir," said Joe. "But you've got it off your chest, anyway."

Mr. Lavender regarded him for a moment in silence; then putting his hand to his throat, said hoarsely:

"No, on my chest, I think, Joe. All public speakers do. It is inseparable from that great calling."

"'Alf a mo'!" grunted Joe, diving into the recesses beneath the driving-seat. "'Ere, swig that off, sir."

Mr. Lavender raised the tumbler of fluid to his mouth, and drank it off; only from the dregs left on his moustache did he perceive that it smelled of rum and honey.

"Joe," he said reproachfully, "you have made me break my pledge."

Joe smiled. "Well, what are they for, sir? You'll sleep at 'ome to-night."

"Never," said Mr. Lavender. "I shall sleep at High Barnet; I must address them there tomorrow on abstinence during the war."

"As you please, sir. But try and 'ave a nap while we go along." And lifting Blink into the car, where she lay drenched and exhausted by excitement, with the petal of a purple flower clinging to her black nose, he mounted to his seat and drove off. Mr. Lavender, for years unaccustomed to spirituous liquor, of which he had swallowed nearly half a pint neat, passed rapidly into a state of coma. Nor did he fully regain consciousness till he awoke in bed the next morning.

IV

INTO THE DANGERS OF A PUBLIC LIFE

"At what time is my meeting?" thought Mr. Lavender vaguely, gazing at the light filtering through the Venetian blind. "Blink!"

His dog, who was lying beside his bed gnawing a bone which with some presence of mind she had brought in, raised herself and regarded him with the innocence of her species. "She has an air of divine madness," thought Mr. Lavender, "which is very pleasing to me. I have a terrible headache." And seeing a bellrope near his hand he pulled it.

A voice said: "Yes, sir."

"I wish to see my, servant, Joe Petty," said Lavender. "I shall not require any breakfast thank you. What is the population of High Barnet?"

"I'm sure I don't know what you're talking about, sir," answered the voice, which seemed to be that of his housekeeper; "but you can't see Joe; he's gone out with a flea in his ear. The idea of his letting you get your feet wet like that!"

"How is this?" said Mr. Lavender. "I thought you were

the chambermaid of the inn at High Barnet?"

"No, indeed," said Mrs. Petty soothingly, placing a thermometer in his mouth. "Smoke that a minute, sir. Oh! look at what this dog's brought in! Fie!" And taking the bone between thumb and finger she cast it out of the window; while Blink, aware that she was considered in the wrong, and convinced that she was in the right, spread out her left paw, laid her head on her right paw, and pressed her chin hard against it. Mrs. Petty, returning from the window, stood above her master, who lay gazing up with the thermometer jutting out through the middle of his moustache.

"I thought so!" she said, removing it; "a hundred and one. No getting up for you, sir! That Joe!"

"Mrs. Petty," said Mr. Lavender rather feebly, for his head pained him excessively, "bring me the morning papers."

"No, sir. The thermometer bursts at an an' ten. I'll bring you the doctor."

Mr. Lavender was about to utter a protest when he reflected that all public men had doctors.

"About the bulletin?" he said faintly.

"What?" ejaculated Mrs. Petty, whose face seemed to Mr. Lavender to have become all cheekbones, eyes, and shadows. Joe never said a about a bullet. Where? and however did you get it in?

"I did not say 'bullet in'," murmured Mr. Lavender closing his eyes! "I said bulletin. They have it."

At this mysterious sentence Mrs. Petty lifted her hands, and muttering the word "Ravin'!" hastened from the room. No sooner had she gone, however, than Blink, whose memory was perfect, rose, and going to the window placed her forepaws on the sill. Seeing her bone shining on the lawn below, with that disregard of worldly consequence which she shared with all fine characters, she leaped through. The rattle of the Venetian blind disturbed Mr. Lavender from the lethargy to which he had reverted. "Mr. John Lavender passed a good night," he thought, "but his condition is still critical." And in his disordered imagination he seemed to see people outside Tube stations, standing stock-still in the middle of the traffic, reading that bulletin in the evening papers. "Let me see," he mused, "how will they run? To-morrow I shall be better, but not yet able to leave my bed; the day after to-morrow I shall have a slight relapse, and my condition will still give cause for anxiety; on the day following - What is that noise. For a sound like the whiffling of a wind through dry sticks combined with the creaking of a saw had, impinged on his senses. It was succeeded by scratching. "Blink!" said Mr. Lavender. A heartrending whine came from outside the door. Mr. Lavender rose and opened it. His dog came in carrying her bone, and putting it down by the bed divided her attention between it and her master's legs, revealed by the night-shirt which, in deference to the great Disraeli, he had never abandoned in favour of pyjamas. Having achieved so erect a posture Mr. Lavender, whose heated imagination had now carried him to the convalescent stage of his indisposition, felt that a change of air would do him good, and going to the window, leaned out above a lilac-tree.

"Mr. John Lavender," he murmured, "has gone to his

seat to recuperate before resuming his public duties."

While he stood there his attention was distracted by a tall young lady of fine build and joyous colour, who was watering some sweet-peas in the garden of the adjoining castle: Naturally delicate, Mr. Lavender at once sought a jacket, and, having put it on, resumed his position at the window. He had not watched her more than two minutes before he saw that she was cultivating soil, and, filled with admiration, he leaned still further out, and said:

"My dear young madam, you are doing a great work."

Thus addressed, the young lady, who had those roving grey eyes which see everything and betoken a large nature not devoid of merry genius, looked up and smiled.

"Believe me," continued Mr. Lavender, "no task in these days is so important as the cultivation of the soil; now that we are fighting to the last man and the last dollar every woman and child in the islands should put their hands to the plough. And at that word his vision became feverishly enlarged, so that he seemed to see not merely the young lady, but quantities of young ladies, filling the whole garden.

"This," he went on, raising his voice, "is the psychological moment, the turning-point in the history of these islands. The defeat of our common enemies imposes on us the sacred duty of feeding ourselves once more. 'There is a tide in the affairs of men which taken at the flood leads on to -- Oh!" For in his desire to stir his audience, Mr. Lavender had reached out too far, and losing foothold on his polished bedroom floor, was slipping down into the lilac-bush. He was arrested by a jerk from behind; where Blink, moved by this sudden elopement of her master, had seized him by the nightshirt tails, and was staying his descent.

"Is anything up?" said the young lady.

"I have lost my balance," thickly answered Mr. Lavender, whose blood was running to his head, which was now lower than his feet." Fortunately, my dog seems to be holding me from behind. But if someone could assist her it would be an advantage, for I fear that I am slipping."

"Hold on!" cried the young lady. And breaking through the low privet hedge which separated the domains, she vanished beneath him with a low gurgling sound.

Mr. Lavender, who dared not speak again for fear that Blink, hearing his voice, might let go to answer, remained suspended, torn with anxiety about his costume. "If she comes in," he thought, "I shall die from shame. And if she doesn't, I shall die from a broken neck. What a dreadful alternative! And he firmly grasped the most substantial lilac-boughs within, his reach, listening with the ears of a hare for any sound within the room, in which he no longer was to any appreciable extent. Then the thought of what a public man should feel in his position came to his rescue. "We die but once," he mused; "rather than shock that charming lady let me seek oblivion." And the words of his obituary notice at once began to dance before his eyes. "This great public servant honoured his country no less in his death than in his life.' Then striking out vigorously with his feet he launched his body forward. The words "My goodness resounded above him, as all restraining influence was suddenly relaxed; Mr. Lavender slid into the lilac-bush, turned heels over head, and fell bump on the ground. He lay there at full, length, conscious of everything, and especially of the faces of Blink and the young lady looking down on him from the window.

"Are you hurt?" she called.

"No," said Mr. Lavender that is - er - yes," he added, ever scrupulously exact.

"I'm coming down," said the young lady.

"Don't move!"

With a great effort Mr. Lavender arranged his costume, and closed his eyes. "How many lie like this, staring at the blue heavens!" he thought.

"Where has it got you?" said a voice; and he saw the young lady bending over him.

"'In the dorsal region, I think," said Mr. Lavender. "But I suffer more from the thought that I - that you - "

"That's all right," said the young lady; "I'm a V.A.D. It WAS a bump! Let's see if you can -- " and taking his hands she raised him to a sitting posture. "Does it work?"

"Yes," said Mr. Lavender rather faintly.

"Try and stand," said the young lady, pulling.

Mr. Lavender tried, and stood; but no, sooner was he

on his feet than she turned her face away. Great tears rolled down her cheeks; and she writhed and shook all over.

"Don't!" cried Mr. Lavender, much concerned. "I beg you not to cry. It's nothing, I assure you - nothing!" The young lady with an effort controlled her emotion, and turned her large grey eyes on him.

"The angelic devotion of nurses!" murmured Mr. Lavender, leaning against the wall of the house with his hand to his back. "Nothing like it has been seen since the world began."

"I shall never forget the sight!" said the young lady, choking.

Mr. Lavender, who took the noises she made for sobbing, was unutterably disturbed.

"I can't bear to see you distressed on my account," he said. "I am quite well, I assure you; look - I can walk!" And he started forth up the garden in his nightshirt and Norfolk jacket. When he turned round she was no longer there, sounds of uncontrollable emotion were audible from the adjoining garden. Going to the privet hedge, he looked aver. She was lying gracefully on the grass, with her face smothered in her hands, and her whole body shaking. "Poor thing!" thought Mr. Lavender. "No doubt she is one of those whose nerves have been destroyed by the terrible sights she has seen!" But at that moment the young lady rose and ran as if demented into her castle. Mr. Lavender stayed transfixed. "Who would not be ill for the pleasure of drinking from a cup held by her hand?" he thought. "I am fortunate to have received injuries in trying to save

John Glasworthy

her from confusion. Down, Blink, down!"

For his dog, who had once more leaped from the window, was frantically endeavouring to lick his face. Soothing her, and feeling his anatomy, Mr. Lavender became conscious that he was not alone. An old lady was standing on the gardenpath which led to the front gate, holding in her hand a hat. Mr. Lavender sat down at once, and gathering his nightshirt under him, spoke as follows:

"There are circumstances, madam, which even the greatest public servants cannot foresee, and I, who am the humblest of them, ask you to forgive me for receiving you in this costume."

"I have brought your hat back," said the old lady with a kindling eye; "they told me you lived here and I was anxious to know that you and your dear dog were none the worse."

"Madam," replied Mr. Lavender, "I am infinitely obliged to you. Would you very kindly hang my, hat up on the - er - weeping willow tree?"

At this moment a little white dog, who accompanied the old lady, began sniffing round Mr. Lavender, and Blink, wounded in her proprietary instincts, placed her paws at once on her master's shoulders, so that he fell prone. When he recovered a sitting posture neither the old lady nor the little dog were in sight, but his hat was hanging on a laurel bush. "There seems to be something fateful about this morning," he mused; "I had better go in before the rest of the female population -- " and recovering his feet with difficulty, he took his hat, and was about to enter the house when he saw the young lady watching him from an upper window of the adjoining castle. Thinking to relieve her anxiety, he said at once:

"My dear young lady, I earnestly beg you to believe that such a thing never happens to me, as a rule."

Her face was instantly withdrawn, and, sighing deeply, Mr. Lavender entered the house and made his way upstairs. "Ah!" he thought, painfully recumbent in his bed once more, "though my bones ache and my head burns I have performed an action not unworthy of the traditions of public life. There is nothing more uplifting than to serve Youth and Beauty at the peril of one's existence. Humanity and Chivalry have ever been the leading characteristics of the British race;" and, really half-delirious now, he cried aloud: "This incident will for ever inspire those who have any sense of beauty to the fulfilment of our common task. Believe me, we shall never sheathe the sword until the cause of humanity and chivalry is safe once more."

Blink, ever uneasy about sounds which seemed to her to have no meaning, stood up on her hind legs and endeavoured to stay them by licking his face; and Mr. Lavender, who had become so stiff that he could not stir without great pain, had to content himself by moving his head feebly from side to side until his dog, having taken her fill, resumed the examination of her bone. Perceiving presently that whenever he began to-talk she began to lick his face, he remained silent, with his mouth open and his eyes shut, in an almost unconscious condition, from which he was roused by a voice saying:

"He is suffering from alcoholic poisoning."

The monstrous injustice of these words restored his faculties, and seeing before him what he took to be a large concourse of people - composed in reality of Joe Petty, Mrs. Petty, and the doctor - he thus addressed them in a faint, feverish voice:

"The pressure of these times, ladies and gentlemen, brings to the fore the most pushing and obstreperous blackguards. We have amongst us persons who, under the thin disguise of patriotism, do not scruple to bring hideous charges against public men. Such but serve the blood-stained cause of our common enemies. Conscious of the purity of our private lives, we do not care what is said of us so long as we can fulfil our duty to our country. Abstinence from every form of spirituous liquor has been the watchword of all public men since this land was first threatened by the most stupendous cataclysm which ever hung over the heads of a great democracy. We have never ceased to preach the need for it, and those who say the contrary are largely Germans or persons lost to a sense of decency." So saying, he threw off all the bedclothes, and fell back with a groan.

"Easy, easy, my dear sir!" said the voice.

"Have you a pain in your back?"

"I shall not submit," returned our hero, "to the ministrations of a Hun; sooner will I breathe my last."

"Turn him over," said the voice. And Mr. Lavender found himself on his face.

"Do you feel that?" said the voice.

Mr. Lavender answered faintly into his pillow:

"It is useless for you to torture me. No German hand shall wring from me a groan."

"Is there mania in his family?" asked the voice. At this cruel insult Mr. Lavender, who was nearly smothered, made a great effort, and clearing his mouth of the pillow, said:

"Since we have no God nowadays, I call the God of my fathers to witness that there is no saner public man than I."

It was, however, his last effort, for the wriggle he had given to his spine brought on a kind of vertigo, and he relapsed into unconsciousness.

V

IS CONVICTED OF A NEW DISEASE

Those who were assembled round the bed of Mr. Lavender remained for a moment staring at him with their mouths open, while Blink growled faintly from underneath.

"Put your hand here," said the doctor at last.

"There is a considerable swelling, an appearance of inflammation, and the legs are a curious colour. You gave him three-quarters of a tumbler of rum - how much honey?"

Thus addressed, Joe Petty, leaning his head a little to one side, answered:

"Not 'alf a pot, sir."

"Um! There are all the signs here of something quite new. He's not had a fall, has he?"

"Has he?" said Mrs. Petty severely to her husband.

"No," replied Joe.

"Singular!" said the doctor. Turn him back again; I

want to feel his head. Swollen; it may account for his curious way of talking. Well, shove in quinine, and keep him quiet, with hot bottles to his feet. I think we have come on a new war disease. I'll send you the quinine. Good morning.

"Wot oh!" said Joe to his wife, when they were left alone with the unconscious body of their master. "Poor old Guv! Watch and pray!"

"However could you have given him such a thing?"

"Wet outside, wet your inside," muttered Joe sulkily, "'as always been my motto. Sorry I give 'im the honey. Who'd ha' thought the product of an 'armless insect could 'a done 'im in like this?"

Fiddle said Mrs. Petty. "In my belief it's come on through reading those newspapers. If I had my way I'd bum the lot. Can I trust you to watch him while I go and get the bottles filled?"

Joe drooped his lids over his greenish eyes, and, with a whisk of her head, his wife left the room.

"Gawd 'elp us!" thought Joe, gazing at his unconscious master, and fingering his pipe; "'ow funny women are! If I was to smoke in 'ere she'd have a fit. I'll just 'ave a whiff in the window, though!" And, leaning out, he drew the curtains to behind him and lighted his pipe.

The sound of Blink gnawing her bone beneath the bed alone broke the silence.

"I could do with a pint o' bitter," thought Joe; and, noticing the form of the weekly gardener down below, he said softly:

"'Ello, Bob!"

"'Ello?" replied the gardener. "'Ow's yours?"

"Nicely."

"Goin' to 'ave some rain?"

"Ah!"

"What's the, matter with that?"

"Good for the crops."

"Missis well?"

"So, so."

"Wish mine was."

"Wot's the matter with her?"

"Busy!" replied Joe, sinking his voice. Never 'ave a woman permanent; that's my experience.

The gardener did not reply, but stood staring at the lilac-bush below Joe Petty's face. He was a thin man, rather like an old horse.

"Do you think we can win this war?" resumed Joe.

"Dunno," replied the gardener apathetically.

"We seem to be goin' back nicely all the time."

Joe wagged his head. "You've 'it it," he said. And, jerking his head back towards the room behind him, "Guv'nor's got it now."

"What?"

"The new disease."

"What new disease?"

"Wy, the Run-abaht-an-tell-'em-'ow-to-do-it."

"Ah!"

"'E's copped it fair. In bed."

"You don't say!"

"Not 'alf!" Joe sank his voice still lower. "Wot'll you bet me I don't ketch it soon?"

The gardener uttered a low gurgle.

"The cats 'ave been in that laylock," he replied, twisting off a broken branch. "I'll knock off now for a bit o' lunch."

But at that moment the sound of a voice speaking as it might be from a cavern, caused him and Joe Petty to stare at each other as if petrified.

"Wot is it?" whispered Joe at last.

The gardener jerked his head towards a window on the ground floor.

"Someone in pain," he said.

"Sounds like the Guv'nor's voice."

"Ah!" said the gardener.

"Alf a mo'!" And, drawing in his head, Joe peered through the curtains. The bed was empty and the door open.

"Watch it! 'E's loose!" he called to the gardener, and descended the stairs at a run.

In fact, Mr. Lavender had come out of his coma at the words, " D'you think we can win this war?" And, at once conscious that he had not read the morning papers, had got out of bed. Sallying forth just as he was he had made his way downstairs, followed by Blink. Seeing the journals lying on the chest in the hall, he took all five to where he usually went at this time of the morning, and sat down to read. Once there, the pain he was in, added to the disorder occasioned in his brain by the five leaders, caused him to give forth a summary of their contents, while Blink pressed his knees with her chin whenever the rising of his voice betokened too great absorption, as was her wont when she wanted him to feed her. Joe Petty joined the gardener in considerable embarrassment.

"Shan't I not 'alf cop it from the Missis?" he murmured. "The door's locked."

The voice of Mr. Lavender maintained its steady flow, rising and falling with the tides of his pain and his feelings. "What, then, is our duty? Is it not plain and simple? We require every man in the Army, for that is the 'sine qua non' of victory. We must greatly reinforce the ranks of labour in our shipyards - ships, ships, ships, always more ships; for without them we shall infallibly be defeated. We cannot too often repeat that we must see the great drama that is being played before our eyes steadily, and we must see it whole.... Not a man must be taken from the cultivation of our soil, for on that depends our very existence as a nation. Without abundant labour of the right sort on the land we cannot hope to cope with the menace of the pirate submarine. We must have the long vision, and not be scuppered by the fears of those who would deplete our most vital industry . . . . In munition works," wailed Mr. Lavender's voice, as he reached the fourth leader, "we still require the maximum of effort, and a considerable reinforcement of manpower will in that direction be necessary to enable us to establish the 'overwhelming superiority in the air and in guns which alone can ensure the defeat of our enemies".... He reached the fifth in what was almost a scream. "Every man up to sixty must be mobilized but here we would utter the most emphatic caveat. In the end this war will be won by the country whose financial position stands the strain best. The last copper bullet will be the deciding factor. Our economic strength must on no account be diminished. We cannot at this time of day afford to deplete the ranks of trade and let out the very life-blood in our veins. "We must see," groaned Mr. Lavender, "the problem steadily, and see it whole."

"Poor old geyser!" said the gardener; "'e do seem bad."

"Old me!" said Joe.

"I'll get on the sill and see what I can do through the top o' the window."

He got up, and, held by the gardener, put his arm through. There was the sound of considerable disturbance, and through the barking of Blink, Mr. Lavender's voice was heard again: "Stanch in the middle of the cataclysm, unruffled by the waters of heaven and hell, let us be captains of our souls. Down, Blink, down!"

"He's out!" said Joe, rejoining the gardener. "Now for it, before my missis comes!" and he ran into the house.

Mr. Lavender was walking dazedly in the hall with the journals held out before him.

"Joe," he said, catching sight of his servant, "get the car ready. I must be in five places at once, for only thus can we defeat the greatest danger which ever threatened the future of civilization."

"Right-o, sir," replied Joe; and, waiting till his master turned round, he seized him round the legs, and lifting that thin little body ascended the stairs, while Mr. Lavender, with the journals waving fanlike in his hands, his white hair on end, and his legs kicking, endeavoured to turn his head to see what agency was moving him.

At the top of the stairs they came on Mrs. Petty, who, having Scotch blood in her veins, stood against the wall to let them pass, with a hot bottle in either hand. Having placed Mr. Lavender in his bed and drawn the clothes up to his eyes, Joe Petty passed the back of his hand across his brow, and wrung it out.

"Phew!" he gasped; "he's artful!"

His wife, who had followed them in, was already fastening her eyes on the carpet.

"What's that?" she said, sniffing.

"That?" repeated Joe, picking up his pipe; "why, I had to run to ketch 'im, and it fell out o' me pocket."

"And lighted itself," said Mrs. Petty, darting, at the floor and taking up a glowing quid which had burned a little round hole in the carpet. "You're a pretty one!"

"You can't foresee those sort o' things," said Joe.

"You can't foresee anything," replied his wife; "you might be a Government. Here! hold the clothes while I get the bottles to his feet. Well I never! If he hasn't got -- " And from various parts of Mr. Lavender's body she recovered the five journals. "For putting things in the wrong place, Joe Petty, I've never seen your like!"

"They'll keep 'im warm," said Joe.

Mr. Lavender who, on finding himself in bed, had once more fallen into a comatose condition, stirred, and some words fell from his lips. "Five in one, and one in five."

"What does he say?" said Mrs. Petty, tucking him up.

"It's the odds against Candelabra for the Derby."

"Only faith," cried Mr. Lavender, "can multiply exceedingly."

"Here, take them away!" muttered Mrs. Petty, and

dealing the journals a smart slap, she handed them to Joe.

"Faith!" repeated Mr. Lavender, and fell into a doze.

"About this new disease," said Joe. "D'you think it's ketchin'? I feel rather funny meself."

"Stuff!" returned his wife. "Clear away those papers and that bone, and go and take Blink out, and sit on a seat; it's all you're fit for. Of all the happy-go-luckys you're the worst."

"Well, I never could worry," said Joe from the doorway; "'tisn't in me. So long!"

And, dragging Blink by the collar, he withdrew.

Alone with her patient, Mrs. Petty, an enthusiast for cleanliness and fresh air, went on her knees, and, having plucked out the charred ring of the little hole in the carpet, opened the window wider to rid the room of the smell of burning. "If it wasn't for me," she thought, leaning out into the air, "I don't know what'd become of them."

A voice from a few feet away said:

"I hope he's none the worse. What does the doctor say?"

Looking round in astonishment, Mrs. Petty saw a young lady leaning out of a window on her right.

"We can't tell at present," she said, with a certain reserve he is going on satisfactory.

"It's not hydrophobia, is it?" asked the young lady. "You know he fell out of the window?

"What!" ejaculated Mrs. Petty.

"Where the lilac's broken. If I can give you a hand I shall be very glad. I'm a V.A.D."

"Thank you, I'm sure," said Mrs. Petty stiffly, for the passion of jealousy, to which she was somewhat prone, was rising in her, "there is no call." And she thought, "V.A. indeed! I know them."

Poor dear said the young lady. "He did come a bump. It was awfully funny! Is he - er -- ?" And she touched her forehead, where tendrils of fair hair were blowing in the breeze.

Inexpressibly outraged by such a question concerning one for whom she had a proprietary reverence, Mrs. Petty answered acidly:

"Oh dear no! He is much wiser than some people!"

"It was only that he mentioned the last man and the last dollar, you know," said the young lady, as if to herself, "but, of course, that's no real sign." And she uttered a sudden silvery laugh.

Mrs. Petty became aware of something tickling her left ear, and turning round, found her master leaning out beside her, in his dressing-gown.

Leave me, Mrs. Petty," he said with such dignity that she instinctively recoiled. "It may seem to you," continued Mr. Lavender, addressing the young lady, "indelicate on my part to resume my justification, but as a public man, I suffer, knowing that I have committed a breach of decorum."

"Don't you think you ought to keep quiet in bed?" Mrs. Petty heard the young lady ask.

"My dear young lady, "Mr. Lavender replied, "the thought of bed is abhorrent to me at a time like this. What more ignoble fate than to die in, one's bed?

"I'm only asking you to live in it," said the young lady, while Mrs. Petty grasped her master by the skirts of his gown.

"Down, Blink, down!" said Mr. Lavender, leaning still further out.

"For pity's sake, "wailed the young lady, don't fall out again, or I shall burst."

"Ah, believe me," said Mr. Lavender in a receding voice, "I would not pain you further for the world -- "

Mrs. Petty, exerting all her strength, had hauled him in.

"Aren't you ashamed of yourself, sir," she said severely, "talking to a young lady like that in your dressing-gown?

"Mrs. Petty," said Mr Lavender mysteriously, "it might have been worse.... I should like some tea with a little lemon in it."

Taking this for a sign of returning reason Mrs. Petty drew him gently towards the bed, and, having seen him get in, tucked him up and said:

"Now, sir, you never break your word, do you?"

"No public man -- " began Mr. Lavender.

"Oh, bother! Now, promise me to stay quiet in bed while I get you that tea."

"I certainly shall," replied our hero, "for I feel rather faint."

"That's right," said Mrs. Petty. "I trust you." And, bolting the window, she whisked out of the room and locked the door behind her.

Mr. Lavender lay with his eyes fixed on the, ceiling, clucking his parched tongue. "God," he thought, "for one must use that word when the country is in danger - God be thanked for Beauty! But I must not allow it to unsteel my soul. Only when the cause of humanity has triumphed, and with the avenging sword and shell we have exterminated that criminal nation, only then shall I be entitled to let its gentle influence creep about my being." And drinking off the tumbler of tea which Mrs. Petty was holding to his lips, he sank almost immediately into a deep slumber.

VI

MAKES A MISTAKE, AND MEETS A MOON-CAT

The old lady, whose name was Sinkin, and whose interest in Mr. Lavender had become so deep, lived in a castle in Frognal; and with her lived her young nephew, a boy of forty-five, indissolubly connected with the Board of Guardians. It was entirely due to her representations that he presented himself at Mr. Lavender's on the following day, and, sending in his card, was admitted to our hero's presence.

Mr. Lavender, pale and stiff, was sitting in his study, with Blink on his feet, reading a speech.

"Excuse my getting up, sir," he said; "and pray be seated."

The nephew, who had a sleepy, hairless face and little Chinese eyes, bowed, and sitting down, stared at Mr. Lavender with a certain embarrassment.

"I have come," he said at last, "to ask you a few questions on behalf of -- "

"By all means," said Mr. Lavender, perceiving at once that he was being interviewed. "I shall be most happy to give you my views. Please take a cigarette, for I believe that is usual. I myself do not smoke. If it is the human touch you want, you may like to know that I gave it up when that appeal in your contemporary flooded the trenches with cigarettes and undermined the nerves of our heroes. By setting an example of abstinence, and at the same time releasing more tobacco for our men, I felt that I was but doing my duty. Please don't mention that, though. And while we are on the personal note, which I sincerely deprecate, you might like to stroll round the room and look at the portrait of my father, behind the door, and of my mother, over the fireplace. Forgive my not accompanying you. The fact is - this is an interesting touch - I have always been rather subject to lumbago." And seeing the nephew Sinkin, who had risen to his suggestion, standing somewhat irresolutely in front of him, he added: "Perhaps you would like to look a little more closely at my eyes. Every now and then they flash with an almost uncanny insight." For by now he had quite forgotten his modesty in the identification he felt with the journal which was interviewing him. "I am fifty-eight," he added quickly; "but I do not look my years, though my hair, still thick and full of vigour, is prematurely white - so often the case with men whose brains are. continually on the stretch. The little home, far from grandiose, which forms the background to this most interesting personality is embowered in trees. Cats have made their mark on its lawns, and its owner's love of animals was sharply illustrated by the sheep-dog which lay on his feet clad in Turkish slippers. Get up, Blink!"

Blink, disturbed by the motion of her master's feet, rose and gazed long into his face.

"Look!" said Mr. Lavender," she has the most beautiful

eyes in the world."

At this remark, which appeared to him no saner than the others he had heard - so utterly did he misjudge Mr. Lavender's character - the nephew put down the notebook he had taken out of his pocket, and said:

"Has there ever been anything - er - remarkable about your family?"

"Indeed, yes," said Mr. Lavender. Born of poor but lofty parentage in the city of Rochester, my father made his living as a publisher; my mother was a true daughter of the bards, the scion of a stock tracing its decent from the Druids; her name was originally Jones."

"Ah!" said the nephew Sinkin, writing.

"She has often told me at her knee," continued Mr. Lavender, "that there was a strong vein of patriotism in her family."

"She did not die - in - in -- "

"No, indeed," interrupted Mr. Lavender; she is still living there."

"Ah!" said the nephew. "And your brothers and sisters?"

"One of my brothers," replied Mr. Lavender, with pardonable pride, "is the editor of Cud Bits. The other is a clergyman."

"Eccentric," murmured the nephew absently. "Tell me,

Mr. Lavender, do you find your work a great strain? Does it -- " and he touched the top of his head, covered with moist black hair.

Mr. Lavender sighed. "At a time like this," he said, "we must all be prepared to sacrifice our health. No public man, as you know, can call his head his own for a moment. I should count myself singularly lacking if I stopped to consider - er - such a consideration."

Consider - er - such a consideration," repeated the nephew, jotting it down.

"He carries on," murmured Mr. Lavender, once more identifying himself with the journal, "grappling with the intricacies of this enormous problem; happy in the thought that nothing - not even reason itself - is too precious to sacrifice on the altar of his duty to his country. The public may rest confident in the knowledge that he will so carry on till they carry him out on his shield." And aware subconsciously that the interview could go no further than that phrase, Mr. Lavender was silent, gazing up with rather startled eyes.

"I see," said the nephew; "I am very much obliged to you. Is your dog safe?" For Blink had begun to growl in a low and uneasy manner.

"The gentlest creature in the world," replied Lavender, "and the most sociable. I sometimes think," he went on in a changed voice, "that we have all gone mad, and that animals alone retain the sweet reasonableness which used to be esteemed a virtue in human society. Don't take that down," he added quickly, "we are all subject to moments of weakness. It was just an 'obiter dictum'."

"Make your mind easy," said the nephew, rising, "it does not serve my purpose. Just one thing, Mr. Lavender."

At this moment Blink, whose instinct had long been aware of some sinister purpose in this tall and heavy man, whose trousers did not smell of dogs, seeing him approach too near, bit him gently in the calf.

The nephew started back. "She's bitten me!" he said, in a hushed voice.

"My God!" ejaculated Mr. Lavender and falling back again, so stiff was he. "Is it possible? There must be some good reason. Blink!"

Blink wagged her little tail, thrust her nose into his hand, removed it, and growled again.

"She is quite well, I assure you," Mr. Lavender added hastily, "her nose is icy."

"She's bitten me," repeated the nephew, pulling up his trouser leg. "There's no mark, but she distinctly bit me."

"Treasure!" said Mr. Lavender, endeavouring to interest him in the dog. "Do you notice how dark the rims of her eyes are, and how clear the whites? Extraordinarily well bred. Blink!"

Aware that she was being talked of Blink continued to be torn between the desire to wag her tail and to growl. Unable to make up her mind, she sighed heavily and fell on her side against her side against her master's legs.

"Wonderful with sheep, too," said Mr. Lavender; "at least, she would be if they would let her.... You should see her with them on the Heath. They simply can't bear her."

"You will hear from me again," said the nephew sourly.

"Thank you," said Mr. Lavender. "I shall be glad of a proof; it is always safer, I believe."

"Good morning," said the nephew.

Blink, who alone perceived the dark meaning in these words, seeing him move towards the door began to bark and run from side to side behind him, for all the world as if he had been a flock of sheep.

"Keep her off!" said the nephew anxiously. "Keep her off. I refuse to be bitten again."

"Blink!" called Mr. Lavender in some agony. Blink, whose obedience was excessive, came back to him at once, and stood growling from under her master's hand, laid on the white hair which flowed back from her collar, till the nephew's footsteps had died away. "I cannot imagine," thought Mr. Lavender, "why she should have taken exception to that excellent journalist. Perhaps he did not smell quite right? One never knows."

And with her moustachioed muzzle pressed to his chin Mr. Lavender sought for explanation in the innocent and living darkness of his dog's eyes....

On leaving Mr. Lavender's the nephew forthwith returned to the castle in Frognal, and sought his aunt.

"Mad as a March hare, Aunt Rosie; and his dog bit me."

"That dear doggie?"

"They're dangerous."

"You were always funny about dogs, dear, said his aunt soothingly." Why, even Sealey doesn't really like you. "And calling to the little low white dog she quite failed to attract his attention. "Did you notice his dress. The first time I took him for a shepherd, and the second time --! What do you think ought to be done?"

"He'll have to be watched," said the nephew. "We can't have lunatics at large in Hampstead."

"But, Wilfred," said the old lady, "will our man-power stand it? Couldn't they watch each other? Or, if it would be any help, I could watch him myself. I took such a fancy to his dear dog."

"I shall take steps," said the nephew.

"No, don't do that. I'll go and call on the people, next door. Their name is Scarlet. They'll know about him, no doubt. We mustn't do anything inconsiderate."

The nephew, muttering and feeling his calf, withdrew to his study. And the old lady, having put on her bonnet, set forth placidly, unaccompanied by her little white dog.

On arriving at the castle embedded in acacias and laurustinus she asked of the maid who opened:

"Can I see Mrs. Scarlet?"

"No," replied the girl dispassionately; "she's dead."

"Mr. Scarlet, then?"

"No," replied the girl he's a major."

"Oh, dear!" said the old lady.

"Miss Isabel's at home," said the girl, who appeared, like so many people in time of war, to be of a simple, plain-spoken nature; "you'll find her in the garden." And she let the old lady out through a French window.

At the far end, under an acacia, Mrs. Sinkin could see the form of a young lady in a blue dress, lying in a hammock, with a cigarette between her lips and a yellow book in her hands. She approached her thinking, "Dear me! how comfortable, in these days!" And, putting her head a little on one side, she said with a smile: "My name is Sinkin. I hope I'm not disturbing you."

The young lady rose with a vigorous gesture.

"Oh, no! Not a bit."

"I do admire some people," said the old lady; "they seem to find time for everything."

The young lady stretched herself joyously.

"I'm taking it out before going to my new hospital. Try it," she said touching the hammock; "it's not bad. Will you have a cigarette?"

"I'm afraid I'm too old for both," said the old lady, "though I've often thought they must be delightfully soothing. I wanted to speak to you about your neighbour."

The young lady rolled her large grey eyes. "Ah!" she said, "he's perfectly sweet."

"I know," said the old lady, "and has such a dear dog. My nephew's very interested in them. You may have heard of him - Wilfred Sinkin - a very clever man; on so many Committees."

"Not really?" said the young lady.

"Oh, yes! He has one of those heads which nothing can disturb; so valuable in these days."

"And what sort of a heart?" asked the young lady, emitting a ring of smoke.

"Just as serene. I oughtn't to say so, but I think he's rather a wonderful machine."

"So long as he's not a doctor! You can't think how they get on your nerves when they're, like that. I've bumped up against so many of them. They fired me at last!"

"Really? Where? I thought they only did that to the dear horses. Oh, what a pretty laugh you have! It's so pleasant to hear anyone laugh, in these days."

"I thought no one did anything else! I mean, what else can you do, except die, don't you know?"

"I think that's rather a gloomy view," said the old lady placidly. But about your neighbour. What is his name?"

"Lavender. But I call him Don Pickwixote."

"Dear me, do you indeed? Have you noticed anything very eccentric about him?"

"That depends on what you call eccentric. Wearing a nightshirt, for instance? I don't know what your standard is, you see."

The old lady was about to reply when a voice from the adjoining garden was heard saying:

"Blink! Don't touch that charming mooncat!"

"Hush!" murmured the young lady; and seizing her visitor's arm, she drew her vigorously beneath the acacia tree. Sheltered from observation by those thick and delicate branches, they stooped, and applying their eyes to holes in the privet hedge, could see a very little cat, silvery-fawn in colour and far advanced in kittens, holding up its paw exactly like a dog, and gazing with sherry-coloured eyes at Mr. Lavender, who stood in the middle of his lawn, with Blink behind him.

"If you see me going to laugh," whispered the young lady, "pinch me hard."

"Moon-cat," repeated Mr. Lavender, "where have you come from? And what do you want, holding up your paw like that? What curious little noises you make, duckie!" The cat, indeed, was uttering sounds rather like a duck. It came closer to Mr. Lavender, circled his legs, drubbed itself against Blink's chest, while its tapered tail, barred with silver, brushed her mouth.

"This is extraordinary," they heard Mr. Lavender say; "I would stroke it if I wasn't so stiff. How nice of you little moon-cat to be friendly to my play-girl! For what is there in all the world so pleasant to see as friendliness between a dog and cat!"

At those words the old lady, who was a great lover of animals, was so affected that she pinched the young lady by mistake.

"Not yet!" whispered the latter in some agony. "Listen!"

"Moon-cat," Mr. Lavender was saying, "Arcadia is in your golden eyes. You have come, no doubt, to show us how far we have strayed away from it." And too stiff to reach the cat by bending, Mr. Lavender let himself slowly down till he could sit. "Pan is dead," he said, as he arrived on the grass and crossed his feet, "and Christ is not alive. Moon-cat!"

The little cat had put its head into his hand, while Blink was thrusting her nose into his mouth.

"I'm going to sneeze!" whispered the old lady, strangely affected.

"Pull your upper lip down hard, like the German

Empress, and count nine!" murmured the young.

While the old lady was doing this Mr. Lavender had again begun to speak.

"Life is now nothing but explosions. Gentleness has vanished, and beauty is a dream. When you have your kittens, moon-cat, bring them up in amity, to love milk, dogs, and the sun."

The moon-cat, who had now reached his shoulder, brushed the tip of her tail across his loose right eyebrow, while Blink's jealous tongue avidly licked his high left cheekbone. With one hand Mr. Lavender was cuddling the cat's head, with the other twiddling Blink's forelock, and the watchers could see his eyes shining, and his white hair standing up all ruffled.

"Isn't it sweet?" murmured the old lady.

"Ah! moon-cat," went on Mr. Lavender, "come and live with us. You shall have your kittens in the bathroom, and forget this age of blood and iron."

Both the old lady and the young were removing moisture from their eyes when, the voice of Mr. Lavender, very changed, recalled them to their vigil. His face had become strained and troubled.

"Never," he was saying, "will we admit that doctrine of our common enemies. Might is not right gentlemen those who take the sword shall perish by the sword. With blood and iron we will ourselves stamp out this noxious breed. No stone shall be left standing, and no babe sleeping in that abandoned country. We will restore the tide of humanity, if we have to wade through rivers of blood across mountains of iron."

"Whom is he calling gentlemen?" whispered the old lady.

But Blink, by anxiously licking Mr. Lavender's lips, had produced a silence in which the young-lady did not dare reply. The sound of the little cat's purring broke the hush.

"Down, Blink, down!" said Mr. Lavender.

"Watch this little moon-cat and her perfect manners! We may all learn from her how not to be crude. See the light shining through her pretty ears!"

The little cat, who had seen a bird, had left Mr. Lavender's shoulder, and was now crouching and moving the tip of its tail from side to side.

"She would like a bird inside her; but let us rather go and find her some milk instead," said Mr. Lavender, and he began to rise.

"Do you know, I think he's quite sane, whispered the old lady, "except, perhaps, at intervals. What do you?"

"Glorious print!" cried Mr. Lavender suddenly, for a journal had fallen from his pocket, and the sight of it lying there, out of his reach, excited him. "Glorious print! I can read you even from here. When the enemy of mankind uses the word God he commits blasphemy! How different from us!" And raising his eyes from the journal Mr. Lavender fastened them, as it seemed to his anxious listeners, on the tree which sheltered them. "Yes! Those unseen presences, who search out the workings of our heart, know that even the most Jingo among us can say, 'I am not as they are!' Come, mooncat!"

So murmuring, he turned and moved towards the house, clucking with his tongue, and followed by Blink.

"Did he mean us?" said the old lady nervously.

"No; that was one of his intervals. He's not mad; he's just crazy."

"Is there any difference, my dear?"

"Why, we're all crazy about something, you know; it's only a question of what."

"But what is his what?"

"He's got a message. They're in the air, you know."

"I haven't come across them," said the old lady. "I fear I live a very quiet life - except for picking over sphagnum moss."

"Oh, well! There's no hurry."

"Well, I shall tell my nephew what I've seen," said the old lady. "Good-bye."

"Good-bye," responded the young; and, picking up her yellow book, she got back into the hammock and relighted her cigarette.

VII

SEES AND EDITOR, AND FINDS A FARMER

Not for some days after his fall from the window did Mr. Lavender begin to regain the elasticity of body necessary to the resumption of public life. He spent the hours profitably, however, in digesting the newspapers and storing ardour. On Tuesday morning, remembering that no proof of his interview had yet been sent him, and feeling that he ought not to neglect so important a matter, he set forth to the office of the great journal from which, in the occult fashion of the faithful, he was convinced the reporter had come. While he was asking for the editor in the stony entrance, a young man who was passing looked at him attentively and said: "Ah, sir, here you are! He's waiting for you. Come up, will you?"

Mr. Lavender followed up some stairs, greatly gratified at the thought that he was expected. The young man led him through one or two swing doors into an outer office, where a young woman was typing.

Mr. Lavender shook his head, and sat down on the edge of a green leather chair. The editor, resuming his seat, crossed his legs deferentially, and sinking his chin again on his chest, began:

"About your article. My only trouble, of course, is that I'm running that stunt on British prisoners - great success! You've seen it, I suppose?"

"Yes, indeed," said Mr. Lavender; I read you every day.

The editor made a little movement which showed that he was flattered, and sinking his chin still further into his chest, resumed:

"It might run another week, or it might fall down tomorrow - you never can tell. But I'm getting lots of letters. Tremendous public interest."

"Yes, yes," assented Mr. Lavender, "it's most important."

"Of course, we might run yours with it," said the editor. "But I don't know; I think it'd kill the other. Still -- "

"I shouldn't like -- " began Mr. Lavender.

"I don't believe in giving them more than they want, you know," resumed the editor. "I think I'll have my news editor in," and he blew into a tube. "Send me Mr. Crackamup. This thing of yours is very important, sir. Suppose we began to run it on Thursday. Yes, I should think they'll be tired of British prisoners by then."

"Don't let me," began Mr. Lavender.

The editor's eye became unveiled for the Moment. "You'll be wanting to take it somewhere else if we -- Quite! Well, I think we could run them together. See here, Mr. Crackamup" - Mr. Lavender saw a small man like Beethoven frowning from behind spectacles - "could we run this German prisoner stunt alongside the British, or d'you think it would kill it?"

Mr. Lavender almost rose from his chair in surprise. "Are you -- " he said; "is it -- "

The small man hiccoughed, and said in a raw voice:

"The letters are falling off."

"Ah!" murmured the editor, "I thought we should be through by Thursday. We'll start this new stunt Thursday. Give it all prominence, Crackamup. It'll focus fury. All to the good - all to the good. Opinion's ripe." Then for a moment he seemed to hesitate, and his chin sank back on his chest. "I don't know," he murmured of course it may -- "

"Please," began Mr. Lavender, rising, while the small man hiccoughed again. The two motions seemed to determine the editor.

"That's all right, sir," he said, rising also; "that's quite all right. We'll say Thursday, and risk it. Thursday, Crackamup. "And he held out his hand to Mr. Lavender. "Good morning, sir, good morning. Delighted to have seen you. You wouldn't put your name to it? Well, well, it doesn't matter; only you could have written it. The turn of phrase - immense! They'll tumble all right!" And Mr. Lavender found himself, with Mr. Crackamup, in the lobby. "It's bewildering," he thought, "how quickly he settled that. And yet he had such repose. But is there some mistake?" He was about to ask his companion, but with a distant hiccough the small man had vanished. Thus deserted, Mr. Lavender was in two minds whether to ask to be readmitted, when the four gentlemen with notebooks repassed him in single file into the editor's room.

"My name is Lavender," he said resolutely to the young woman. "Is that all right?"

"Quite," she answered, without looking up.

Mr. Lavender went out slowly, thinking, "I may perhaps have said more in that interview than I remember. Next time I really will insist on having a proof. Or have they taken me for some other public man?" This notion was so disagreeable, however, that he dismissed it, and passed into the street.

On Thursday, the day fixed for his fresh tour of public speaking, he opened the great journal eagerly. Above the third column was the headline: OUR VITAL DUTY: BY A GREAT PUBLIC MAN. "That must be it," he thought. The article, which occupied just a column of precious space, began with an appeal so moving that before he had read twenty lines Mr. Lavender had identified himself completely with the writer; and if anyone had told him that he had not uttered these sentiments, he would have given him the lie direct. Working from heat to heat the article finished in a glorious outburst with a passionate appeal to the country to starve all German prisoners.

Mr. Lavender put it down in a glow of exultation. "I shall translate words into action," he thought; "I shall at once visit a rural district where German prisoners are working on the land, and see that the farmers do their duty. "And, forgetting in his excitement to eat his breakfast, he put the journal in his pocket, wrapped himself in his dust-coat and broad-brimmed hat, and went out to his car, which was drawn up, with Blink, who had not forgotten her last experience, inside.

"We will go to a rural district, Joe," he said, getting in.

"Very good, sir," answered Joe; and, unnoticed by the population, they glided into the hazy heat of the June morning.

"Well, what abaht it, sir?" said Joe, after they had proceeded for some three hours. "Here we are."

Mr. Lavender, who had been lost in the beauty of the scenes through which he was passing, awoke from reverie, and said:

"I am looking for German prisoners, Joe; if you see a farmer, you might stop."

"Any sort of farmer?" asked Joe.

"Is there more than one sort?" returned Mr. Lavender, smiling.

Joe cocked his eye. "Ain't you never lived in the country, sir?"

"Not for more than a few weeks at a time, Joe, unless Rochester counts. Of course, I know Eastbourne very well."

"I know Eastbourne from the inside," said Joe discursively. "I was a waiter there once."

"An interesting life, a waiter's, Joe, I should think."

"Ah! Everything comes to 'im who waits, they say. But abaht farmers - you've got a lot to learn, sir."

"I am always conscious of that, Joe; the ramifications of public life are innumerable."

"I could give you some rummikins abaht farmers. I once travelled in breeches."

"You seem to have done a great many things Joe."

"That's right, sir. I've been a sailor, a 'traveller,' a waiter, a scene-shifter, and a shover, and I don't know which was the cushiest job. But, talking of farmers: there's the old English type that wears Bedfords - don't you go near 'im, 'e bites. There's the modern scientific farmer, but it'll take us a week to find 'im. And there's the small-'older, wearin' trahsers, likely as not; I don't think 'e'd be any use to you.

"What am I to do then?" asked Mr Lavender.

"Ah!" said Joe, "'ave lunch."

Mr. Lavender sighed, his hunger quarelling with his sense of duty. "I should like to have found a farmer first," he said.

"Well, sir, I'll drive up to that clump o'beeches, and you can have a look round for one while I get lunch ready.

"That will do admirably."

There's just one thing, sir," said Joe, when his master was about to start; "don't you take any house you come across for a farm. They're mostly cottages o' gentility nowadays, in'abited by lunatics."

"I shall be very careful," said Mr. Lavender.

"This glorious land!" he thought, walking away from the beech clump, with Blink at his heels; "how wonderful to see it being restored to its former fertility under pressure of the war! The farmer must be a happy man, indeed, working so nobly for his country, without thought of his own prosperity. How flowery those beans look already!" he mused, glancing at a field of potatoes. "Now that I am here I shall be able to combine my work on German prisoners with an effort to stimulate food production. Blink!" For Blink was lingering in a gateway. Moving back to her, Mr. Lavender saw that the sagacious animal was staring through the gate at a farmer who was standing in a field perfectly still, with his back turned, about thirty yards away.

"Have you -- " Mr. Lavender began eagerly; "is it - are you employing any
German prisoners, sir?"

The farmer did not seem to hear. "He must," thought Mr. Lavender, "be of the old stolid English variety."

The farmer, who was indeed attired in a bowler hat and Bedford cords, continued to gaze over his land, unconscious of Mr. Lavender's presence.

"I am asking you a question, sir," resumed the latter in a louder voice." And however patriotically absorbed you may be in cultivating your soil, there is no necessity for rudeness."

The farmer did not move a muscle.

"Sir," began Mr. Lavender again, very patiently, "though I have always heard that the British farmer is of all men least amenable to influence and new ideas, I have never believed it, and I am persuaded that if you will but listen I shall be able to alter your whole outlook about the agricultural future of this country." For it had suddenly occurred to him that it might be a long time before he had again such an opportunity of addressing a rural audience on the growth of food, and he was loth to throw away the chance. The farmer, however, continued to stand with his hack to the speaker, paying no more heed to his voice than to the buzzing of a fly.

"You SHALL hear me," cried Mr. Lavender, unconsciously miming a voice from the past, and catching, as he thought, the sound of a titter, he flung his hand out, and exclaimed:

"Grass, gentlemen, grass is the hub of the matter. We have put our hand to the plough" - and, his imagination taking flight at those words, he went on in a voice calculated to reach the great assembly of farmers which he now saw before him with their backs turned - "and never shall we take it away till we have reduced every acre in the country to an arable condition. In the future not only must we feed ourselves, but our dogs, our horses, and our children, and restore the land to its pristine glory in the front rank of the world's premier industry. But me no buts," he went on with a winning smile, remembering that geniality is essential in addressing a country audience, "and butter me no butter, for in future we shall require to grow our margarine as well. Let us, in a word, put behind us all prejudice and pusillanimity till we see this country of ours once more blooming like one great cornfield, covered with cows. Sirs, I am no iconoclast; let us do all this without departing in any way from those great principles of Free Trade, Industrialism, and Individual Liberty which have made our towns the largest, most crowded, and wealthiest under that sun which never sets over the British Empire. We do but need to see this great problem steadily and to see it whole, and we shall achieve this revolution in our national life without the sacrifice of a single principle or a single penny. Believe me, gentlemen, we shall yet eat our cake and have it."

Mr. Lavender paused for breath, the headlines of his great speech in tomorrow's paper dancing before his eyes: "THE CLIMACTERIC - EATS CAKE AND HAS IT - A GREAT CONCLUSION." The wind, which had risen somewhat during Mr. Lavender's speech, fluttered the farmer's garments at this moment, so that they emitted a sound like the stir which runs through an audience at a moment of strong emotion.

"Ah!" cried Mr. Lavender, "I see that I move you, gentlemen. Those have traduced you who call you unimpressionable. After all, are you not the backbone of this country up which runs the marrow which feeds the brain; and shall you not respond to an appeal at once so simple and so fundamental? I assure you, gentlemen, it needs no thought; indeed, the less you think about it the better, for to do so will but weaken your purpose and distract your attention. Your duty is to go forward with stout hearts, firm steps, and kindling eyes; in this way alone shall we defeat our common enemies. And at those words, which he had uttered at the top of his voice, Mr. Lavender stood like a clock which has run down, rubbing his eyes. For Blink, roaming the field during the speech, and encountering quadruped called rabbit, which she had never seen before, had backed away from it in dismay, brushed against the farmer's legs and caused his breeches to fall down, revealing the sticks on which they had been draped. When Mr. Lavender saw this he called out in a loud voice Sir, you have deceived me. I took you for a human being. I now perceive that you are but a selfish automaton, rooted to your own business, without a particle of patriotic sense. Farewell!"

VIII

STARVES SOME GERMANS

After parting with the scarecrow Mr. Lavender who felt uncommonly hungry' was about to despair of finding any German prisoners when he saw before him a gravel-pit, and three men working therein. Clad in dungaree, and very dusty, they had a cast of countenance so unmistakably Teutonic that Mr. Lavender stood still. They paid little or no attention to him, however, but went on sadly and silently with their work, which was that of sifting gravel. Mr. Lavender sat down on a milestone opposite, and his heart contracted within him. "They look very thin and sad," he thought, "I should not like to be a prisoner myself far from my country, in the midst of a hostile population, without a woman or a dog to throw me a wag of the tail. Poor men! For though it is necessary to hate the Germans, it seems impossible to forget that we are all human beings. This is weakness," he added to himself, "which no editor would tolerate for a moment. I must fight against it if I am to fulfil my duty of rousing the population to the task of starving them. How hungry they look already - their checks are hollow! I must be firm. Perhaps they have wives and families at home, thinking of them at this moment. But, after all, they are Huns. What did the great writer say? 'Vermin - creatures no more worthy of pity than the tiger or the rat.' How true! And yet - Blink!" For his dog, seated on her haunches, was looking at him with that peculiarly steady gaze which betokened in her the desire for food. "Yes," mused Mr. Lavender, "pity is the mark of the weak man. It is a vice which was at one time rampant in this country; the war has made one beneficial change at least - we are moving more and more towards the manly and unforgiving vigour of the tiger and the rat. To be brutal! This is the one lesson that the Germans can teach us, for we had almost forgotten the art. What danger we were in! Thank God, we have past masters again among us now!" A frown became fixed between his brows. "Yes, indeed, past masters. How I venerate those good journalists and all the great crowd of witnesses who have dominated the mortal weakness, pity. 'The Hun must and shall be destroyed - root and branch - hip and thigh - bag and baggage man, woman, and babe - this is the sole duty of the great and humane British people. Roll up, ladies and gentlemen, roll up! Great thought - great language! And yet -- "

Here Mr. Lavender broke into a gentle sweat, while the Germans went on sifting gravel in front of him, and Blink continued to look up into his face with her fixed, lustrous eyes. "What an awful thing," he thought, "to be a man. If only I were just a public man and could, as they do, leave out the human and individual side of everything, how simple it would be! It is the being a man as well which is so troublesome. A man has feelings; it is wrong - wrong! There should be no connection whatever between public duty and the feelings of a man. One ought to be able to starve one's enemy without a quiver, to watch him drown without a wink. In fact, one ought to be a German. We ought all to be Germans. Blink, we ought all to be Germans, dear! I must steel myself!" And Mr. Lavender wiped his forehead, for, though a great idea had come to him, he still lacked the heroic savagery to put it into execution. "It is my duty," he thought, "to cause those hungry, sad-looking men to follow me and watch me eat my lunch. It is my duty. God give me strength! For unless I make this sacrifice of my gentler nature I shall be unworthy to call myself a public man, or to be reported in the newspapers. 'En avant, de Bracy!'" So musing, he rose, and Blink with him. Crossing the road, he clenched his fists, and said in a voice which anguish made somewhat shrill:

"Are you hungry, my friends?"

The Germans stopped sifting gravel, looked up at him, and one of them nodded.

"And thirsty?"

This time they all three nodded.

"Come on, then," said Mr. Lavender.

And he led the way back along the road, followed by Blink and the three Germans. Arriving at the beech clump whose great trees were already throwing shadows, denoting that it was long past noon, Mr. Lavender saw that Joe had spread food on the smooth ground, and was, indeed, just finishing his own repast.

"What is there to eat?" thought Mr. Lavender, with a soft of horror. "For I feel as if I were about to devour a meal of human flesh." And he looked round at the three Germans slouching up shamefacedly behind him.

"Sit down, please," he said. The three men sat down.

"Joe," said Mr. Lavender to his surprised chauffeur, "serve my lunch. Give me a large helping, and a glass of ale. "And, paler than his holland dust-coat, he sat resolutely down on the bole of a beech, with Blink on her haunches beside him. While Joe was filling a plate with pigeon-pie and pouring out a glass of foaming Bass, Mr. Lavender stared at the three Germans and suffered the tortures of the damned. "I will not flinch," he thought; "God helping me, I certainly will not flinch. Nothing shall prevent my going through with it." And his eyes, more prominent than a hunted rabbit's, watched the approach of Joe with the plate and glass. The three men also followed the movements of the chauffeur, and it seemed to Mr. Lavender that their eyes were watering. "Courage!" he murmured to himself, transfixing a succulent morsel with his fork and conveying it to his lips. For fully a minute he revolved the tasty mouthful, which he could not swallow, while the three men's eyes watched him with a sort of lugubrious surprise. "If," he thought with anguish, "if I were a prisoner in Germany! Come, come! One effort, it's only the first mouthful!" and with a superhuman effort, he swallowed. "Look at me!" he cried to the three Germans, "look at me! I - I - I'm going to be sick!" and putting down his plate, he rose and staggered forward. "Joe," he said in a dying voice, "feed these poor men, feed them; make them drink; feed them!" And rushing headlong to the edge of the grove, he returned what he had swallowed - to the great interest of Brink. Then, waving away the approach of Joe, and consumed with shame and remorse at his lack of heroism, he ran and hid himself in a clump of hazel bushes, trying to slink into the earth. "No," he thought; "no; I am not for public life. I have failed at the first test. Was ever so squeamish an exhibition? I have betrayed my country and the honour of public life. These Germans are now full of beer and pigeon-pie. What am I but a poltroon, unworthy to lace the shoes of the great leaders of my land? The sun has witnessed my disgrace."

How long he stayed there lying on his face he did not know before he heard the voice of Joe saying, "Wot oh, sir!"

"Joe," replied Mr. Lavender faintly, "my body is here, but my spirit has departed."

"Ah!" said Joe, "a rum upset - that there. Swig this down, sir!" and he held out to his master, a flask-cup filled with brandy. Mr. Lavender swallowed it.

"Have they gone?" he said, gasping.

"They 'ave, sir," replied Joe, "and not 'alf full neither. Where did you pick 'em up?"

"In a gravel-pit," said Mr. Lavender. "I can never forgive myself for this betrayal of my King and country. I have fed three Germans. Leave me, for I am not fit to mingle with my fellows."

"Well, I don't think," said Joe. "Germans?"

Gazing up into his face Mr. Lavender read the unmistakable signs of uncontrolled surprise.

"Why do you look at me like that?" he said.

"Germans?" repeated Joe; "what Germans? Three

blighters workin' on the road, as English as you or me. Wot are you talkin' about, sir?"

"What!" cried Mr. Lavender do you tell me they were not Germans?"

"Well, their names was Tompkins, 'Obson, and Brown, and they 'adn't an 'aitch in their 'eads."

"God be praised said Mr. Lavender. "I am, then, still an English gentleman. Joe, I am very hungry; is there nothing left?"

"Nothin' whatever, sir," replied Joe.

"Then take me home," said Mr. Lavender; "I care not, for my spirit has come back to me."

So saying, he rose, and supported by Joe, made his way towards the car, praising God in his heart that he had not disgraced his country.

IX

CONVERSES WITH A CONSCIENTIOUS OBJECTOR

"Yes," said Mr. Lavender, when they had proceeded some twenty miles along the road for home, "my hunger is excessive. If we come across an hotel, Joe, pull up."

"Right-o, sir," returned Joe. "'Otels, ain't what they were, but we'll find something. I've got your coupons."

Mr. Lavender, who was seated beside his chauffeur on the driving-seat, while Blink occupied in solitude the body of the car, was silent for a minute, revolving a philosophic thought.

"Do you find," he said suddenly, "that compulsory sacrifice is doing you good, Joe?"

"It's good for my thirst, sir," replied Joe. "Never was so powerful thirsty in me life as I've been since they watered beer. There's just 'enough in it to tickle you. That bottle o' Bass you would 'ave 'ad at lunch is the last of the old stock at 'ome, sir; an' the sight of it fair gave me the wind up. To think those blighters 'ad it! Wish I'd known they was Germans - I wouldn't 'ave weakened on it."

"Do not, I beg," said Mr. Lavender, "remind me of that episode. I sometimes think," he went on as dreamily as his hunger would permit, "that being forced to deprive oneself awakens one's worst passions; that is, of course, speaking rather as a man than a public man. What do you think will happen, Joe, when we are no longer obliged to sacrifice ourselves?

"Do wot we've been doin all along - sacrifice someone else," said Joe lightly.

"Be serious, Joe," said Mr. Lavender.

"Well," returned Joe, "I don't know what'll 'appen to you, sir, but I shall go on the bust permanent."

Mr. Lavender sighed. "I do so wonder whether I shall, too," he said.

Joe looked round at him, and a gleam of compassion twinkled in his greenish eyes. "Don't you worry, sir," he said; "it's a question of constitootion. A week'd sew you up."

"A week!" said Mr. Lavender with watering lips, "I trust I may not forget myself so long as that. Public men do not go 'on the bust,' Joe, as you put it."

"Be careful, sir! I can't drive with one eye."

"How can they, indeed?" went on Mr. Lavender; "they are like athletes, ever in training for their unending conflict with the national life."

"Well," answered Joe indulgently, "they 'as their own kind of intoxication, too - that's true; and the fumes is permanent; they're gassed all the time, and chloroformed the rest.

"I don't know to what you allude, Joe," said Mr. Lavender severely.

"'Aven't you never noticed, sir, that there's two worlds - the world as it is, and the world as it seems to the public man?"

"That may be," said Mr. Lavender with some excitement. "But which is the greater, which is the nobler, Joe? And what does the other matter? Surely that which flourishes in great minds, and by their utterances is made plain. Is it not better to live in a world where nobody shrinks from being starved or killed so long as they can die for their kings and countries, rather than in a world where people merely wish to live?"

"Ah!" said Joe, "we're all ready to die for our countries if we've got to. But we don't look on it, like the public speakers, as a picnic. They're a bit too light-'earted."

"Joe," said Mr. Lavender, covering his ears, and instantly uncovering them again, "this is the most horrible blasphemy I have ever listened to."

"I can do better than that, sir," answered Joe. "Shall I get on with it?"

"Yes," said Mr. Lavender, clenching his hands, "a public man shrinks from nothing - not even from the gibes of his enemies."

"Well, wot abaht it, sir? Look at the things they say,

and at what really is. Mind you, I'm not speakin' particular of the public men in this country - or any other country; I'm speakin' of the lot of 'em in every country. They're a sort of secret society, brought up on gas. And every now and then someone sets a match to it, and we get it in the neck. Look 'ere, sir. Dahn squats one on his backside an' writes something in 'igh words. Up pops another and says something in 'igher; an' so they go on poppin' up an' squattin' dahn till you get an atmosphere where you can't breathe; and all the time all we want is to be let alone, and 'uman kindness do the rest. All these fellers 'ave got two weaknesses - one's ideas, and the other's their own importance. They've got to be conspicuous, and without ideas they can't, so it's a vicious circle. When I see a man bein' conspicuous, I says to meself: 'Gawd 'elp us, we shall want it!' And sooner or later we always do. I'll tell you what's the curse of the world, sir; it's the gift of expressin' what ain't your real feeling. And - Lord! what a lot of us 'ave got it!"

"Joe," said Mr. Lavender, whose eyes were almost starting from his head, "your words are the knell of poetry, philosophy, and prose - especially of prose. They are the grave of history, which, as you know, is made up of the wars and intrigues which have originated in the brains of public men. If your sordid views were true, how do you suppose for one minute that in this great epic struggle we could be consoled by the thought that we are 'making history'? Has there been a single utterance of any note which has not poured the balm of those words into our ears? Think how they have sustained the widow and the orphan, and the wounded lying out in agony under the stars. 'To make history,' 'to act out the great drama' - that thought, ever kept before us, has been our comfort and their stay. And you would take it from us? Shame - shame!" repeated Mr. Lavender. You would destroy all glamour, and be the death of every principle."

"Give me facts," said Joe stubbornly, "an' you may 'ave my principles. As to the other thing, I don't know what it is, but you may 'ave it, too. And 'ere's another thing, sir: haven't you never noticed that when a public man blows off and says something, it does 'im in? No matter what 'appens afterwards, he's got to stick to it or look a fool."

"I certainly have not," said Mr. Lavender. I have never, or very seldom, noticed that narrowness in public men, nor have I ever seen them 'looking fools' as you rudely put it."

"Where are your eyes, sir?" answered Joe; "where are your eyes? I give you my word it's one or the other, though I admit they've brought camouflage to an 'igh art. But, speaking soberly, sir, if that's possible, public men are a good thing' and you can 'ave too much of it. But you began it, sir," he added soothingly, "and 'ere's your hotel. You'll feel better with something inside you."

So saying, he brought the car to a standstill before a sign which bore the words, "Royal Goat."

Mr. Lavender, deep sunk in the whirlpool of feeling which had been stirred in him by his chauffeur's cynicism, gazed at the square redbrick building with bewildered eyes.

"It's quite O. K.," said Joe; "I used to call here regular when I was travellin' in breeches. Where the commercials are gathered together the tap is good," he added, laying a finger against the side of his nose. "And they've a fine brand of pickles. Here's your coupon."

Thus encouraged, Mr. Lavender descended from the car, and, accompanied by Blink, entered the hotel and sought the coffee-room.

A maid of robust and comely appearance, with a fine free eye, divested him of his overcoat and the coupon, and pointed to a table and a pale and intellectual-looking young man in spectacles who was eating.

"Have you any more beef?" said the latter without looking up.

"No, sir," replied the maid.

"Then bring me the ham and eggs," he added.

"Here's another coupon - and anything else you've got."

Mr. Lavender, whose pangs had leaped in him at the word "beef," gazed at the bare bone of the beef-joint, and sighed.

"I, too, will have some ham and a couple of poached eggs," he said.

"You can have ham, sir," replied the maid, "but there are only eggs enough for one."

"And I am the one," said the young man, looking up for the first time.

Mr. Lavender at once conceived an aversion from him; his appearance was unhealthy, and his eyes ravened from behind the spectacles beneath his high forehead.

"I have no wish to deprive you of your eggs, sir," he said, "though I have had nothing to eat all day."

"I have had nothing to eat to speak of for six months," replied the young man and in a fortnight's time I shall have nothing to eat again for two years."

Mr. Lavender, who habitually spoke, the truth, looked at him with a sort of horror. But the young man had again concentrated his attention on his plate. "How deceptive are appearances," thought Mr. Lavender; "one would say an intellectual, not to say a spiritual type, and yet he eats like a savage, and lies like a trooper!" And the pinchings of his hunger again attacking him, he said rather acidly:

May I ask you, sir, whether you consider it amusing to tell such untruths to a stranger?

The young man, who had finished what was on his plate, paused, and with a faint smile said:

"I spoke figuratively. You, sir, I expect, have never been in prison."

At the word 'prison' Mr. Lavender's natural kindliness reasserted itself at once. "Forgive me," he said gently; "please eat all the ham. I can easily do with bread and cheese. I am extremely sorry you have had that misfortune, and would on no account do anything which might encourage you to incur it again. If it is a question of money or anything of that sort," he went on timidly, "please command me. I abhor prisons; I consider them inhuman; people should only be confined upon their honours."

The young man's eyes kindled behind his spectacles.

"I have been confined," he said, "not upon my honour, but because of my honour; to break it in."

"How is that?" cried Mr. Lavender, aghast, "to break it in?"

"Yes," said the young man, cutting a large slice of bread, "there's no other way of putting it with truth. They want me to go back on my word to go back on my faith, and I won't. In a fortnight's time they'll gaol me again, so I MUST eat - excuse me. I shall want all my strength." And he filled his mouth too full to go on speaking.

Mr. Lavender stared at him, greatly perturbed.

How unjustly I judged him," he thought; and seeing that the maid had placed the end of a ham before him he began carving off what little there was left on it, and, filling a plate, placed it before the young man. The latter thanked him, and without looking up ate rapidly on. Mr. Lavender watched him with beaming eyes. "It's lovely to see him!" he thought; "poor fellow!"

"Where are the eggs?" said the young man suddenly.

Mr. Lavender got up and rang the bell.

"Please bring those eggs for him," he said.

"Yes, sir," said the maid. "And what are you going to have? There's nothing in the house now."

"Oh!" said Mr. Lavender, startled. "A cup of coffee and a slice of bread, thank you. I can always eat at any time."

The maid went away muttering to herself, and bringing the eggs, plumped them down before the young man, who ate them more hastily than words could tell.

"I mean," he said, "to do all I can in this fort-night to build up my strength. I shall eat almost continuously. They shall never break me." And, reaching out, he took the remainder of the loaf.

Mr. Lavender watched it disappear with a certain irritation which he subdued at once. "How selfish of me," he thought, "even to think of eating while this young hero is still hungry."

"Are you, then," he said, "the victim of some religious or political plot?"

"Both," replied the young man, leaning back with a sigh of repletion, and wiping his mouth. "I was released to-day, and, as I said, I shall be court-martialled again to-day fortnight. It'll be two years this time. But they can't break me."

Mr. Lavender gasped, for at the word "courtmartialled" a dreadful doubt had assailed him.

"Are you," he stammered - "you are not - you cannot be a Conscientious Objector?"

"I can," said the young man.

Mr. Lavender half rose in horror.

"I don't approve," he ejaculated; "I do not approve of you."

"Of course not," said the young man with a little smile at once proud and sad, "who does? If you did I shouldn't have to eat like this, nor should I have the consciousness of spiritual loneliness to sustain me. You look on me as a moral outcast, as a leper. That is my comfort and my strength. For though I have a genuine abhorrence of war, I know full well that I could not stick this if it were not for the feeling that I must not and will not lower myself to the level of mere opportunists like you, and sink myself in the herd of men in the street."

At hearing himself thus described Mr. Lavender flushed.

"I yield to no one, he said, "in my admiration of principle. It is because of my principles that I regard you as a -- "

"Shirker," put in the young man calmly. "Go on; don't mince words; we're used to them."

"Yes," said Mr. Lavender, kindling, "a shirker. Excuse me! A renegade from the camp of Liberty, a deserter from the ranks of Humanity, if you will pardon me."

"Say a Christian, and have done with it," said the young man.

"No," said Mr. Lavender, who had risen to his feet, "I will not go so far as that. You are not a Christian, you are a Pharisee. I abhor you."

"And I abhor you," said the young man suddenly. "I am a Christian Socialist, but I refuse to consider you my brother. And I can tell you this: Some day when through our struggle the triumph of Christian Socialism and of Peace is assured, we shall see that you firebrands and jingoes get no chance to put up your noxious heads and disturb the brotherhood of the world. We shall stamp you out. We shall do you in. We who believe in love will take jolly good care that you apostles of hate get all we've had and more - if you provoke us enough that is."

He stopped, for Mr. Lavender's figure had rigidified on the other side of the table into the semblance of one who is about to address the House of Lords.

"I can find here," he cried, "no analogy with religious persecution. This is a simple matter. The burden of defending his country falls equally on every citizen. I know not, and I care not, what promises were made to you, or in what spirit the laws of compulsory service were passed. You will either serve or go to prison till you do. I am a plain Englishman, expressing the view of my plain countrymen."

The young man, tilting back in his chair, rapped on the table with the handle of his dinner-knife.

"Hear, hear!" he murmured.

"And let me tell you this," continued Mr. Lavender, "you have no right to put a mouthful of food between your lips so long as you are not prepared to die for it. And if the Huns came here tomorrow I would not lift a finger to save you from the fate you would undoubtedly receive."

During this colloquy their voices had grown so loud that the maid, entering in dismay, had gone into the bar and informed the company that a Conscientious Objector had eaten all the food and was "carrying on outrageous" in the coffee-room. On hearing this report those who were assembled - being four commercial travellers far gone in liquor - taking up the weapons which came nearest to hand - to wit, four syphons - formed themselves two deep and marched into the coffee-room. Aware at once from Mr. Lavender's white hair and words that he was not the Objector in question, they advanced upon the young man, who was still seated, and taking up the four points of the compass, began squirting him unmercifully with soda-water. Blinded and dripping, the unfortunate young fellow tried desperately to elude the cordon of his persecutors, only to receive a fresh stream in his face at each attempt. Seeing him thus tormented, amid the coarse laughter of these half-drunken "travellers," Mr. Lavender suffered a moment of the most poignant struggle between his principles and his chivalry. Then, almost unconsciously grasping the ham-bone, he advanced and called out loudly:

"Stop! Do not persecute that young man. You are four and he is one. Drop it, I tell you - Huns that you are!"

The commercial fellows, however, laughed; and this infuriating Mr. Lavender, he dealt one of them a blow with the ham-bone, which, lighting on the funny point of his elbow, caused him to howl and spin round the room. One of the others promptly avenged him with a squirt of syphon in Mr. Lavender's left eye; whereon he incontinently attacked them all, whirling the ham-bone round his head like a shillelagh. And had it not been that Blink and the maid seized his coat-tails he would have done them severe injury. It was at this moment that Joe Petty, attracted by the hullabaloo, arrived in the doorway, and running up to his master, lifted him from behind and carried him from the room, still brandishing the ham-bone and kicking out with his legs. Dumping him into the car, Joe mounted hastily and drove off. Mr. Lavender sat for two or three minutes coming to his senses before full realization of what he had done dawned on him. Then, flinging the ham-bone from him, he sank back among the cushions, with his chin buried on his chest. "What have I done?" he thought over and over again. "What have I done? Taken up the bone for a Conscientious Objector - defended a renegade against great odds! My God! I am indeed less than a public man!"

And in this state of utter dejection, inanition, and collapse, with Blink asleep on his feet, he was driven back to Hampstead.

X

DREAMS A DREAM AND SEES A VISION

Though habitually abstemious, Mr. Lavender was so very hungry that evening when he sat down to supper that he was unable to leave the lobster which Mrs. Petty had provided until it was reduced to mere integument. Since his principles prevented his lightening it with anything but ginger-beer he went to bed in some discomfort, and, tired out with the emotions of the day, soon fell into a heavy slumber, which at dawn became troubled by a dream of an extremely vivid character. He fancied himself, indeed, dressed in khaki, with a breastplate composed of newspapers containing reports of speeches which he had been charged to deliver to soldiers at the front. He was passing in a winged tank along those scenes of desolation of which he had so often read in his daily papers, and which his swollen fancy now coloured even more vividly than had those striking phrases of the past, when presently the tank turned a somersault, and shot him out into a morass lighted up by countless star-shells whizzing round and above. In this morass were hundreds and thousands of figures sunk like himself up to the waist, and waving their arms above their heads. "These," thought Mr. Lavender, "must be the soldiers I have come to speak to," and he tore a sheet off his breastplate; but before he could speak from its columns it became thin air in his hand; and he went on tearing off sheet after sheet, hoping to find a speech which would stay solid long enough for him to deliver it. At last a little corner stayed substantial in his hand, and he called out in a loud voice: "Heroes!"

But at the word the figures vanished with a wail, sinking into the mud, which was left covered with bubbles iridescent in the light of the star-shells. At this moment one of these, bursting over his head, turned into a large bright moon; and Mr. Lavender saw to his amazement that the bubbles were really butterflies, perched on the liquid moonlit mud, fluttering their crimson wings, and peering up at him with tiny human faces. "Who are you?" he cried; "oh! who are you?" The butterflies closed their wings; and on each of their little faces came a look so sad and questioning that Mr. Lavender's tears rolled down into his breastplate of speeches. A whisper rose from them. "We are the dead." And they flew up suddenly in swarms, and beat his face with their wings.

Mr. Lavender woke up sitting in the middle of the floor, with light shining in on him through a hole in the curtain, and Blink licking off the tears which were streaming down his face.

"Blink," he said, "I have had a horrible dream." And still conscious of that weight on his chest, as of many undelivered speeches, he was afraid to go back to bed; so, putting on some clothes, he went carefully downstairs and out of doors into the morning. He walked with his dog towards the risen sun, alone in the silvery light of Hampstead, meditating deeply on his dream. "I have evidently," he thought, "not yet acquired that felicitous insensibility which is needful for successful public speaking. This is undoubtedly the secret of my dream. For the sub-conscious knowledge of my deficiency explains the weight on my chest and the futile tearing of sheet after sheet, which vanished as I tore them away. I lack the self-complacency necessary to the orator in any surroundings, and that golden certainty which has enchanted me in the outpourings of great men, whether in ink or speech. This is, however, a matter which I can rectify with practice." And coming to a little may-tree in full blossom, he thus addressed it:

"Little tree, be my audience, for I see in you, tipped with the sunlight, a vision of the tranquil and beautiful world, which, according to every authority, will emerge out of this carnival of blood and iron."

And the little tree lifted up its voice and answered him with the song of a blackbird.

Mr. Lavender's heart, deeply responsive to the voice of Nature, melted within him.

"What are the realms of this earth, the dreams of statesmen, and all plots and policies," he said, "compared with the beauty of this little tree? She - or is it a he? - breathes, in her wild and simple dress, just to be lovely and loved. He harbours the blackbird, and shakes fragrance into the morning; and with her blossom catches the rain and the sun drops of heaven. I see in him the witchery of God; and of her prettiness would I make a song of redemption."

So saying he knelt down before the little tree, while Blink on her haunches, very quiet beside him, looked wiser than many dogs.

A familiar gurgling sound roused him from his devotions, and turning his head he saw his young neighbour in the garb of a nurse, standing on the path behind him. "She has dropped from heaven," he thought for all nurses are angels.

And, taking off his hat, he said:

"You surprised me at a moment of which I am not ashamed; I was communing with Beauty. And behold! Aurora is with me."

"Say, rather, Borealis," said the young lady. "I was so fed-up with hospital that I had to have a scamper before turning in. If you're going home we might go together?"

"It would, indeed, be a joy," said Mr. Lavender. "The garb of mercy becomes you."

"Do you think so?" replied the young lady, in whose cheeks a lovely flush had not deepened. "I call it hideous. Do you always come out and pray to that tree?"

"I am ashamed to say," returned Mr. Lavender, "that I do not. But I intend to do so in future, since it has brought me such a vision."

And he looked with such deferential and shining eyes at his companion that she placed the back of her hand before her mouth, and her breast rose.

"I'm most fearfully sleepy," she said. "Have you had any adventures lately - you and Samjoe?

"Samjoe?" repeated Mr. Lavender.

"Your chauffeur - I call him that. He's very like Sam Weller and Sancho Panza, don't you think, Don Pickwixote?

"Ah!" said Mr. Lavender, bewildered; "Joe, you mean. A good fellow. He has in him the sort of heroism which I admire more than any other."

"Which is that?" asked the young lady.

"That imperturbable humour in the face of adverse circumstances for which our soldiers are renowned."

"You are a great believer in heroics, Don Pickwixote," said the young lady.

"What would life be without them?" returned Mr. Lavender. "The war could not go on for a minute."

"You're right there," said the young lady bitterly.

"You surely," said Mr. Lavender, aghast, cannot wish it to stop until we have destroyed our common enemies?"

"Well," said the young lady," I'm not a Pacifist; but when you see as many people without arms and legs as I do, heroics get a bit off, don't you know." And she increased her pace until Mr. Lavender, who was not within four inches of her stature, was almost compelled to trot. "If I were a Tommy," she added, "I should want to shoot every man who uttered a phrase. Really, at this time of day, they are the limit."

"Aurora," said Mr. Lavender, "if you will permit me, who am old enough - alas! - to be your father, to call you that, you must surely be aware that phrases are the very munitions of war, and certainly not less important than mere material explosives. Take the word 'Liberty,' for instance; would you deprive us of it?"

The young lady fixed on him those large grey eyes which had in them the roll of genius. "Dear Don Pickwixote," she said, "I would merely take it from the mouths of those who don't know what it means; and how much do you think would be left? Not enough to butter the parsnips of a Borough Council, or fill one leader in a month of Sundays. Have you not discovered, Don Pickwixote, that Liberty means the special form of tyranny which one happens to serve under; and that our form of tyranny is GAS."

"High heaven!" cried Mr. Lavender, "that I should hear such words from so red lips!"

"I've not been a Pacifist, so far," continued the young lady, stifling a yawn, "because I hate cruelty, I hate it enough to want to be cruel to it. I want the Huns to lap their own sauce. I don't want to be revengeful, but I just can't help it."

"My dear young lady," said Mr. Lavender soothingly, "you are not - you cannot be revengeful; for every great writer and speaker tells us that revengefulness is an emotion alien to the Allies, who are merely just.

"Rats!"

At this familiar word, Blink who had been following their conversation quietly, threw up her nose and licked the young lady's hand so unexpectedly that she started and added:

"Darling!"

Mr. Lavender, who took the expression as meant for himself, coloured furiously.

"Aurora," he said in a faint voice, "the rapture in my heart prevents my taking advantage of your sweet words. Forgive me, and let us go quietly in, with the vision I have seen, for I know my place."

The young lady's composure seemed to tremble in the balance, and her lips twitched; then holding out her hand she took Mr. Lavender's and gave it a good squeeze.

"You really are a dear," she said. "I think you ought to be in bed. My name's Isabel, you know."

"Not to me," said Mr. Lavender. You are the Dawn; nothing shall persuade me to the contrary. And from henceforth I swear to rise with you every morning."

"Oh, no!" cried the young lady please don't imagine that I sniff the matutinal as a rule. I just happened to be in a night shift."

"No matter," said Mr. Lavender; "I shall see you with the eye of faith, in your night shifts, and draw from the vision strength to continue my public work beckoned by the fingers of the roseate future."

"Well," murmured the young lady, "so long for now; and do go back to bed. It's only about five." And waving the tips of those fingers, she ran lightly up the garden-path and disappeared into her house.

Mr. Lavender remained for a moment as if transfigured; then entering his garden, he stood gazing up at her window, until the thought that she might appear there was too much for him, and he went in.

XI

BREAKS UP A PEACE MEETING

While seated at breakfast on the morning after he had seen this vision, Mr. Lavender, who read his papers as though they had been Holy Writ, came on an announcement that a meeting would be held that evening at a chapel in Holloway under the auspices of the "Free Speakers' League," an association which his journals had often branded with a reputation, for desiring Peace. On reading the names of the speakers Mr. Lavender felt at once that it would be his duty to attend. "There will," he thought, "very likely be no one there to register a protest. For in this country we have pushed the doctrine of free speech to a limit which threatens the noble virtue of patriotism. This is no doubt a recrudescence of that terrible horse-sense in the British people which used to permit everybody to have his say, no matter what he said. Yet I would rather stay at home," he mused "for they will do me violence, I expect; cowardice, however, would not become me, and I must go."

He was in a state of flurry all day, thinking of his unpleasant duty towards those violent persons, and garbishing up his memory by reading such past leaders in his five journals as bore on the subject. He spoke no word of his intentions, convinced that he ran a considerable risk at the hands of the Pacifists, but too sensible of his honour to assist anyone to put that spoke in his wheel which he could not help longing for.

At six o'clock he locked Blink into his study, and arming himself with three leaders, set forth on his perilous adventure. Seven o'clock saw him hurrying along the dismal road to the chapel, at whose door he met with an unexpected check.

"Where is your ticket?" said a large man.

"I have none," replied Mr. Lavender, disconcerted; "for this is a meeting of the Free Speakers' League, and it is for that reason that I have come."

The large man looked at him attentively. "No admittance without ticket," he said.

"I protest," said Mr. Lavender. "How can you call yourselves by that name and not let me in?"

The large man smiled.

"Well, he said, you haven't the strength of - of a rabbit - in you go!"

Mr. Lavender found himself inside and some indignation.

The meeting had begun, and a tall man at the pulpit end, with the face of a sorrowful bull, was addressing an audience composed almost entirely of women and old men, while his confederates sat behind him trying to look as if they were not present. At the end of a row, about half-way up the chapel, Mr. Lavender composed himself to listen, thinking, "However eager I may be to fulfil my duty and break up this meeting, it behoves me as a fair-minded man to ascertain first what manner of meeting it is that I am breaking up." But as the speaker progressed, in periods punctuated by applause from what, by his experience at the door, Mr. Lavender knew to be a packed audience, he grew more and more uneasy. It cannot be said that he took in what the speaker was saying, obsessed as he was by the necessity of formulating a reply, and of revolving, to the exclusion of all else, the flowers and phrases of the leaders which during the day he had almost learned by heart. But by nature polite he waited till the orator was sitting down before he rose, and, with the three leaders firmly grasped in his hand, walked deliberately up to the seated speakers. Turning his back on them, he said, in a voice to which nervousness and emotion lent shrillness:

"Ladies and gentlemen, it is now your turn, in accordance with the tradition of your society, to listen to me. Let us not mince matters with mealy mouths. There are in our midst certain viperous persons, like that notorious gentleman who had the sulphurous impudence to have a French father - French! gentlemen; not German, ladies-mark the cunning and audacity of the fellow; like that renegade Labour leader, who has never led anything, yet, if he had his will, would lead us all into the pit of destruction; like those other high-brow emasculates who mistake their pettifogging pedantry for pearls of price, and plaster the plain issue before us with perfidious and Pacifistic platitudes. We say at once, and let them note it, we will have none of them; we will have -- " Here his words were drowned by an interruption greater even than that; which was fast gathering among the row of speakers behind him, and the surprised audience in front; and he could see the large man being forced from the door and up the aisle by a posse of noisy youths, till he stood with arms pinioned, struggling to turn round, just in front of Mr. Lavender. Seeing his speech thus endangered, the latter cried out at the top of his voice: "Free speech, gentlemen, free speech; I have come here expressly to see that we have nothing of the sort." At this the young men, who now filled the aisle, raised a mighty booing.

"Gentlemen," shouted Mr. Lavender, waving his leaders, "gentlemen --" But at this moment the large man was hurled into contact with what served Mr. Lavender for stomach, and the two fell in confusion. An uproar ensued of which Mr. Lavender was more than vaguely conscious, for many feet went over him. He managed, however, to creep into a corner, and, getting up, surveyed the scene. The young men who had invaded the meeting, much superior in numbers and strength to the speakers, to the large man, and the three or four other able-bodied persons who had rallied to them from among the audience, were taking every advantage of their superiority; and it went to Mr. Lavender's heart to see how they thumped and maltreated their opponents. The sight of their brutality, indeed, rendered him so furious that, forgetting all his principles and his purpose in coming to the meeting, he climbed on to a form, and folding his arms tightly on his breast, called out at the top of his voice:

"Cads! Do not thus take advantage of your numbers. Cads!" Having thus defended what in his calmer moments he would have known to be the wrong, he awaited his own fate calmly. But in the hubbub his words had passed unnoticed. "It is in moments like these," he thought, "that the great speaker asserts his supremacy, quells the storm, and secures himself a hearing." And he began to rack his brains to remember how they did it. "It must require the voice of an ox," he thought, "and the skin of an alligator. Alas! How deficient I am in public qualities!" But his self-depreciation was here cut off with the electric light. At this sheer intervention of Providence Mr. Lavender, listening to the disentangling sounds which rose in the black room, became aware that he had a chance such as he had not yet had of being heard.

"Stay, my friends!" he said; "here in darkness we can see better the true proportions of this great question of free speech. There are some who contend that in a democracy every opinion should be heard; that, just because the good sense of the majority will ever lead the country into the right paths, the minority should be accorded full and fair expression, for they cannot deflect the country's course, and because such expression acts as a healthful safety-valve. Moreover, they say there is no way of preventing the minority from speaking save that of force, which is unworthy of a majority, and the negation of what we are fighting for in this war. But I say, following the great leader-writers, that in a time of national danger nobody ought to say anything except what is in accord with the opinions of the majority; for only in this way can we present a front which will seem to be united to our common enemies. I say, and since I am the majority I must be in the right, that no one who disagrees with me must say anything if we are to save the cause of freedom and humanity. I deprecate violence, but I am thoroughly determined to stand no nonsense, and shall not hesitate to suppress by every means in the power of the majority - including, if need be, Prussian measures - any whisper from those misguided and unpatriotic persons whose so-called principles induce them to assert their right to have opinions of their own. This has ever been a free country, and they shall not imperil its freedom by their volubility and self-conceit." Here Mr. Lavender paused for breath, and in the darkness a faint noise, as of a mouse scrattling at a wainscot, attracted his attention. "Wonderful," he thought, elated by the silence, "that I should so have succeeded in riveting their attention as to be able to hear a mouse gnawing. I must have made a considerable impression." And, fearing to spoil it by further speech, he set to work to grope his way round the chapel wall in the hope of coming to the door. He had gone but a little way when his outstretched hand came into contact with something warm, which shrank away with a squeal.

"Oh!" cried Mr. Lavender, while a shiver went down his spine, "what is that?"

"Me," said a stifled voice. "Who are you?"

"A public speaker, madam," answered Mr. Lavender, unutterably relieved. Don't be alarmed.

"Ouch!" whispered the voice. That madman!

"I assure you, madam," replied Mr. Lavender, striving to regain contact, "I wouldn't harm you for the world. Can you tell me in what portion of the hall we are?" And crouching down he stretched out his arms and felt about him. No answer came; but he could tell that he was between two rows of chairs, and, holding to the top of one, he began to sidle along, crouching, so as not to lose touch with the chairs behind him. He had not proceeded the length of six chairs in the pitchy darkness when the light was suddenly turned up, and he found himself glaring over the backs of the chairs in front into the eyes of a young woman, who was crouching and glaring back over the same chairs.

"Dear me," said Mr. Lavender, as with a certain dignity they both rose to their full height, "I had no conception -- "

Without a word, the young woman put her hand up to her back hair, sidled swiftly down the row of chairs, ran down the aisle, and vanished. There was no one else in the chapel. Mr. Lavender, after surveying the considerable wreckage, made his way to the door and passed out into the night. "Like a dream," he thought; "but I have done my duty, for no meeting was ever more completely broken up. With a clear conscience and a good appetite I can how go home."

XII

SPEEDS UP TRANSPORT, AND SEES A DOCTOR

Greatly cheered by his success at the Peace meeting, Mr. Lavender searched his papers next morning to find a new field for his activities; nor had he to read far before he came on this paragraph:

> Everything is dependent on transport, and we cannot sufficiently urge that this should be speeded up by every means in our power."

"How true!" he thought. And, finishing his breakfast hastily, he went out with Blink to think over what he could do to help. "I can exhort," he mused, "anyone engaged in transport who is not exerting himself to the utmost. It will not be pleasant to do so, for it will certainly provoke much ill-feeling. I must not, however, be deterred by that, for it is the daily concomitant of public life, and hard words break no bones, as they say, but rather serve to thicken the skins and sharpen the tongues of us public men, so that, we are able to meet our opponents with their own weapons. I perceive before me, indeed, a liberal education in just those public qualities wherein I am conscious of being as yet deficient. "And his heart sank within him, thinking of the carts on the hills of Hampstead and the boys who drove them. "What is lacking to them," he mused, "is the power of seeing this problem steadily and seeing it whole. Let me endeavour to impart this habit to all who have any connection with transport."

He had just completed this reflection when, turning a corner, he came on a large van standing stockstill at the top of an incline. The driver was leaning idly against the hind wheel filling a pipe. Mr. Lavender glanced at the near horse, and seeing that he was not distressed, he thus addressed the man:

"Do you not know, my friend, that every minute is of importance in this national crisis? If I could get you to see the question of transport steadily, and to see it whole, I feel convinced that you would not be standing there lighting your pipe when perhaps this half-hour's delay in the delivery of your goods may mean the death of one of your comrades at the front."

The man, who was wizened, weathered, and old, with but few teeth, looked up at him from above the curved hands with which he was coaxing the flame of a match into the bowl of his pipe. His brow was wrinkled, and moisture stood at the corners of his eyes.

"I assure you," went on Mr. Lavender, "that we have none of us the right in these days to delay for a single minute the delivery of anything - not even of speeches. When I am tempted to do so, I think of our sons and brothers in the trenches, and how every shell and every word saves their lives, and I deliver -- "

The old man, who had finished lighting his pipe, took a long pull at it, and said hoarsely:

"Go on!"

"I will," said Mr. Lavender, "for I perceive that I can effect a revolution in your outlook, so that instead of wasting the country's time by leaning against that wheel you will drive on zealously and help to win the war."

The old man looked at him, and one side of his face became drawn up in a smile, which seemed to Mr. Lavender so horrible that he said: "Why do you look at me like that?"

"Cawn't 'elp it," said the man.

"What makes you," continued Mr. Lavender, "pause here with your job half finished? It is not the hill which keeps you back, for you are at the top, and your horses seem rested."

"Yes," said the old man, with another contortion of his face, "they're rested - leastways, one of 'em."

"Then what delays you - if not that British sluggishness which we in public life find such a terrible handicap to our efforts in conducting the war?"

"Ah!" said the old man. "But out of one you don't make two, guv'nor. Git on the offside and you'll see it a bit steadier and a bit 'oler than you 'ave 'itherto."

Struck by his words, which were accompanied by a painful puckering of the checks, Mr. Lavender moved round the van looking for some defect in its machinery, and suddenly became aware that the off horse was lying on the ground, with the traces cut. It lay on its side, and did not move.

"Oh!" cried Mr. Lavender; "oh!" And going up to the horse's head he knelt down. The animal's eye was glazing.

"Oh!" he cried again, "poor horse! Don't die!" And tears dropped out of his eyes on to the horse's cheek. The eye seemed to give him a look, and became quite glazed.

"Dead!" said Mr Lavender in an awed whisper. "This is horrible! What a thin horse - nothing but bones!" And his gaze haunted the ridge and furrow of the horse's carcase, while the living horse looked round and down at its dead fellow, from whose hollow face a ragged forelock drooped in the dust.

"I must go and apologize to that old man," said Mr. Lavender aloud, "for no doubt he is even more distressed than I am."

"Not 'e, guv'nor," said a voice, and looking beside him he saw the aged driver standing beside him; "not 'e; for of all the crool jobs I ever 'ad - drivin' that 'orse these last three months 'as been the croolest. There 'e lies and 'es aht of it; and that's where they'd all like to be. Speed, done 'im in, savin' 'is country's 'time an' 'is country's oats; that done 'im in. A good old 'orse, a willin' old 'orse, 'as broke 'is 'eart tryin' to do 'is bit on 'alf rations. There 'e lies; and I'm glad 'e does." And with the back of his hand the old fellow removed some brown moisture which was trembling on his jaw. Mr. Lavender rose from his knees.

"Dreadful! - monstrous!" he cried; "poor horse! Who is

responsible for this?"

"Why," said the old driver, "the gents as sees it steady and sees it 'ole from one side o' the van, same as you."

So smitten to the heart was Mr. Lavender by those words that he covered his ears with his hands and almost ran from the scene, nor did he stop till he had reached the shelter of his study, and was sitting in his arm-chair with Blink upon his feet. "I will buy a go-cart," he thought, "Blink and I will pull our weight and save the poor horses. We can at least deliver our own milk and vegetables."

He had not been sitting there for half-an-hour revolving the painful complexities of national life before the voice of Mrs. Petty recalled him from that sad reverie.

"Dr. Gobang to see you, sir."

At sight of the doctor who had attended him for alcoholic poisoning Mr. Lavender experienced one or those vaguely disagreeable sensations which follow on half-realized insults.

"Good-morning, sir," said the doctor; thought I'd just look in and make my mind easy about you. That was a nasty attack. Do you still feel your back?"

"No," said Mr. Lavender rather coldly, while Blink growled.

"Nor your head ?"

"I have never felt my head," replied Mr. Lavender, still

more coldly.

"I seem to remember -- " began the doctor.

"Doctor," said Mr. Lavender with dignity, surely you know that public men - do not feel - their heads - it would not do. They sometimes suffer from their throats, but otherwise they have perfect health, fortunately."

The doctor smiled.

"Well, what do you think of the war?" he asked chattily.

"Be quiet, Blink," said Mr. Lavender. Then, in a far-away voice, he added: "Whatever the clouds which have gathered above our heads for the moment, and whatever the blows which Fate may have in store for us, we shall not relax our efforts till we have attained our aims and hurled our enemies back. Nor shall we stop there," he went on, warming at his own words. "It is but a weak-kneed patriotism which would be content with securing the objects for which we began to fight. We shall not hesitate to sacrifice the last of our men, the last of our money, in the sacred task of achieving the complete ruin of the fiendish Power which has brought this great calamity on the world. Even if our enemies surrender we will fight on till we have dictated terms on the doorsteps of Potsdam."

The doctor, who, since Mr. Lavender began to speak, had been looking at him with strange intensity, dropped his eyes.

"Quite so," he said heartily, "quite so. Well, good-morning. I only just ran in!" And leaving Mr. Lavender to the exultation he was evidently feeling, this singular visitor went out and closed the door. Outside the garden-gate he rejoined the nephew Sinkin.

"Well?" asked the latter.

"Sane as you or me," said the doctor. "A little pedantic in his way of expressing himself, but quite all there, really."

"Did his dog bite you?" muttered the nephew. "No," said the doctor absently. "I wish to heaven everyone held his views. So long. I must be getting on." And they parted.

But Mr. Lavender, after pacing the room six times, had sat down again in his chair, with a cold feeling in the pit of his stomach, such as other men feel on mornings after a debauch.

XIII

ADDRESSES SOME SOLDIERS ON THEIR FUTURE

On pleasant afternoons Mr. Lavender would often take his seat on one of the benches which adorned the Spaniard's Road to enjoy the beams of the sun and the towers of the City confused in smoky distance. And strolling forth with Blink on the afternoon of the day on which the doctor had come to see him he sat down to read a periodical, which enjoined on everyone the necessity of taking the utmost interest in soldiers disabled by the war. "Yes," he thought, "it is indeed our duty to force them, no matter what their disablements, to continue and surpass the heroism they displayed out there, and become superior to what they once were." And it seemed to him a distinct dispensation of Providence when the rest of his bench was suddenly occupied by three soldiers in the blue garments and red ties of hospital life. They had been sitting there for some minutes, divided by the iron bars necessary to the morals of the neighbourhood, while Mr. Lavender cudgelled his brains for an easy and natural method of approach, before Blink supplied the necessary avenue by taking her stand before a soldier and looking up into his eye.

"Lord!" said the one thus accosted, "what a fyce! Look

at her moustache! Well, cocky, 'oo are you starin' at?"

"My dog," said Mr. Lavender, perceiving his chance, "has an eye for the strange and beautiful."

"Wow said the soldier, whose face was bandaged, she'll get it 'ere, won't she?"

Encouraged by the smiles of the soldier and his comrades, Mr. Lavender went on in the most natural voice he could assume.

"I'm sure you appreciate, my friends, the enormous importance of your own futures?"

The three soldiers, whose faces were all bandaged, looked as surprised as they could between them, and did not answer. Mr. Lavender went on, dropping unconsciously into the diction of the article he had been reading: "We are now at the turning-point of the ways, and not a moment is to be lost in impressing on the disabled man the paramount necessity of becoming again the captain of his soul. He who was a hero in the field must again lead us in those qualities of enterprise and endurance which have made him the admiration of the world."

The three soldiers had turned what was visible of their faces towards Mr. Lavender, and, seeing that he had riveted their attention, he proceeded: "The apathy which hospital produces, together with the present scarcity of labour, is largely responsible for the dangerous position in which the disabled man now finds himself. Only we who have not to face his future can appreciate what that future is likely to be if he does not make the most strenuous efforts to overcome it.

Boys," he added earnestly, remembering suddenly that this was the word which those who had the personal touch ever employed, "are you making those efforts? Are you equipping your minds? Are you taking advantage of your enforced leisure to place yourselves upon some path of life in which you can largely hold your own against all comers?"

He paused for a reply.

The soldiers, silent for a moment, in what seemed to Mr. Lavender to be sheer astonishment, began to fidget; then the one next him turned to his neighbour, and said:

"Are we, Alf? Are we doin' what the gentleman says?"

"I can answer that for you," returned Mr. Lavender brightly; "for I can tell by your hospitalized faces that you are living in the present; a habit which, according to our best writers, is peculiar to the British. I assure you," he went on with a winning look, "there is no future in that. If you do not at once begin to carve fresh niches for yourselves in the temple of industrialism you will be engulfed by the returning flood, and left high and dry upon the beach of fortune."

During these last few words the half of an irritated look on the faces of the soldiers changed to fragments of an indulgent and protective expression.

"Right you are, guv'nor," said the one in the middle. Don't you worry, we'll see you home all right.

"It is you," said Mr. Lavender, "that I must see home. For that is largely the duty of us who have not had the great privilege of fighting for our country."

These words, which completed the soldiers' conviction that Mr. Lavender was not quite all there, caused them to rise.

"Come on, then," said one; we'll see each other home. We've got to be in by five. You don't have a string to your dog, I see."

"Oh no!" said Mr. Lavender puzzled "I am not blind."

"Balmy," said the soldier soothingly. "Come on, sir, an' we can talk abaht it on the way."

Mr. Lavender, delighted at the impression he had made, rose and walked beside them, taking insensibly the direction for home.

"What do you advise us to do, then, guv'nor?" said one of the soldiers.

"Throw away all thought of the present," returned Mr. Lavender, with intense earnestness; "forget the past entirely, wrap yourselves wholly in the future. Do nothing which will give you immediate satisfaction. Do not consider your families, or any of those transient considerations such as pleasure, your homes, your condition of health, or your economic position; but place yourselves unreservedly in the hands of those who by hard thinking on this subject are alone in the condition to appreciate the individual circumstances of each of you. For only by becoming a flock of sheep can you be conducted into those new pastures where the grass of your future will be sweet and plentiful. Above all, continue to be the heroes which you were under the spur of your country's call, for you must remember that your country is still calling you."

"That's right," said the soldier on Mr. Lavender's left. "Puss, puss! Does your dog swot cats?"

At so irrelevant a remark Mr. Lavender looked suspiciously from left to right, but what there was of the soldiers' faces told him nothing.

"Which is your hospital?" he asked.

"Down the 'ill, on the right," returned the soldier. "Which is yours?"

"Alas! it is not in a hospital that I -- "

"I know," said the soldier delicately, "don't give it a name; no need. We're all friends 'erc. Do you get out much?"

"I always take an afternoon stroll," said Mr. Lavender, "when my public life permits. If you think your comrades would like me to come and lecture to them on their future I should be only too happy."

"D'you 'ear, Alf?" said the soldier. "D'you think they would?"

The soldier, addressed put a finger to the sound side of his mouth and uttered a catcall.

"I might effect a radical change in their views, continued Mr. Lavender, a little puzzled. "Let me leave you this periodical. Read it, and you will see how extremely vital all that I have been saying is. And then, perhaps, if you would send me a round robin, such as is usual in a democratic country, I could pop over almost any day after five. I sometimes feel" - and here Mr. Lavender stopped in the middle of the road, overcome by sudden emotion -- " that I have really no right to be alive when I see what you have suffered for me."

"That's all right, old bean,", said the soldier on his left; "you'd 'a done the same for us but for your disabilities. We don't grudge it you'."

"Boys," said Mr. Lavender, "you are men. I cannot tell you how much I admire and love you."

"Well, give it a rest, then; t'ain't good for yer. And, look 'ere! Any time they don't treat you fair in there, tip us the wink, and we'll come over and do in your 'ousekeeper."

Mr. Lavender smiled.

"My poor housekeeper!" he said. "I thank you all the same for your charming goodwill. This is where I live," he added, stopping at the gate of the little house smothered in lilac and laburnum. "Can I offer you some tea?"

The three soldiers looked at each other, and Mr. Lavender, noticing their surprise, attributed it to the word tea.

"I regret exceedingly that I am a total abstainer," he said.

The remark, completing the soldiers' judgment of his

case, increased their surprise at the nature of his residence; it remained unanswered, save by a shuffling of the feet.

Mr. Lavender took off his hat.

"I consider it a great privilege," he said, "to have been allowed to converse with you. Goodbye, and God bless you!"

So saying, he opened the gate and entered his little garden carrying his hat in his hand, and followed by Blink.

The soldiers watched him disappear within, then continued on their way down the hill in silence.

"Blimy," said one suddenly, "some of these old civilians 'ave come it balmy on the crumpet since the war began. Give me the trenches!"

XIV

ENDEAVOURS TO INTERN A GERMAN

Aglow with satisfaction at what he had been able to do for the wounded soldiers, Mr. Lavender sat down in his study to drink the tea which he found there. "There is nothing in life," he thought, "which gives one such satisfaction as friendliness and being able to do something for others. Moon-cat!"

The moon-cat, who, since Mr. Lavender had given her milk, abode in his castle, awaiting her confinement, purred loudly, regarding him with burning eyes, as was her fashion when she wanted milk, Mr. Lavender put down the saucer and continued his meditations. "Everything is vain; the world is full of ghosts and shadows; but in friendliness and the purring of a little cat there is solidity."

"A lady has called, sir."

Looking up, Mr. Lavender became aware of Mrs. Petty.

"How very agreeable!

"I don't know, sir," returned his housekeeper in her decisive voice; "but she wants to see you. Name of Pullbody."

"Pullbody," repeated Mr. Lavender dreamily; "I don't seem -- Ask her in, Mrs. Petty, ask her in."

"It's on your head, sir," said Mrs. Petty, and went out.

Mr. Lavender was immediately conscious of a presence in dark green silk, with a long upper lip, a loose lower lip, and a fixed and faintly raddled air, moving stealthily towards him.

"Sit down, madam, I beg. Will you have some tea?"

The lady sat down. "Thank you, I have had tea. It was on the recommendation of your next-door neighbour, Miss Isabel Scarlet -- "

"Indeed," replied Mr. Lavender, whose heart began to beat; "command me, for I am entirely at her service."

"I have come to see you," began the lady with a peculiar sinuous smile, "as a public man and a patriot."

Mr. Lavender bowed, and the lady went on: I am in very great trouble. The fact is, my sister's husband's sister is married to a German."

"Is it possible, madam?" murmured Mr. Lavender, crossing his knees, and joining the tips of his fingers.

"Yes," resumed the lady, "and what's more, he is still at large."

Mr. Lavender, into whose mind there had instantly rushed a flood of public utterances, stood gazing at her haggard face in silent sympathy.

"You may imagine my distress, sir, and the condition of my conscience," pursued the lady, "when I tell you that my sister's husband's sister is a very old friend of mine - and, indeed, so was this German. The two are a very attached young couple, and, being childless, are quite wrapped up in each other. I have come to you, feeling it my duty to secure his internment."

Mr. Lavender, moved by the human element in her words, was about to say, "But why, madam?" when the lady continued:

"I have not myself precisely heard him speak well of his country. But the sister of a friend of mine who was having tea in their house distinctly heard him say that there were two sides to every question, and that he could not believe all that was said in the English papers.

"Dear me!" said Mr. Lavender, troubled; "that is serious."

"Yes," went on the lady; "and on another occasion my sister's husband himself heard him remark that a man could not help loving his country and hoping that it would win."

"But that is natural," began Mr. Lavender.

"What!" said the lady, nearly rising, "when that country is Germany?"

The word revived Mr. Lavender's sense of proportion.

"True," he said, "true. I was forgetting for the moment. It is extraordinary how irresponsible one's thoughts are sometimes. Have you reason to suppose that he is dangerous?"

"I should have thought that what I have said might have convinced you," replied the lady reproachfully; "but I don't wish you to act without satisfying yourself. It is not as if you knew him, of course. I have easily been able to get up an agitation among his friends, but I should not expect an outsider - so I thought if I gave you his address you could form your own opinion."

"Yes," murmured Mr. Lavender, "yes. It is in the last degree undesirable that any man of German origin should remain free to work possible harm to our country. There is no question in this of hatred or of mere rabid patriotism," he went on, in a voice growing more and more far-away; it is largely the A. B. C. of common prudence."

"I ought to say," interrupted his visitor, "that we all thought him, of course, an honourable man until this war, or we should not have been his friends. He is a dentist," she added, "and, I suppose, may be said to be doing useful work, which makes it difficult. I suggest that you go to him to have a tooth out."

Mr. Lavender quivered, and insensibly felt his teeth.

"Thank you," he said I will see if I can find one. It is certainly a matter which cannot be left to chance. We public men, madam, often have to do very hard and even inhumane things for no apparent reason. Our consciences alone support us. An impression, I am told, sometimes gets abroad that we yield to clamour.

Those alone who know us realize how unfounded that aspersion is."

"This is his address," said the lady, rising, and handing him an envelope. "I shall not feel at rest until he is safely interned. You will not mention my name, of course. It is tragic to be obliged to work against one's friends in the dark. Your young neighbour spoke in enthusiastic terms of your zeal, and I am sure that in choosing you for my public man she was not pulling - er - was not making a mistake."

Mr. Lavender bowed.

"I hope not, madam, he said humbly I try to do my duty."

The lady smiled her sinuous smile and moved towards the door, leaving on the air a faint odour of vinegar and sandalwood.

When she was gone Mr. Lavender sat down on the edge of his chair before the tea-tray and extracted his teeth while Blink, taking them for a bone, gazed at them lustrously, and the moon-cat between his feet purred from repletion. "There is reason in all things," he thought, running his finger over what was left in his mouth, "but not in patriotism, for that would prevent us from consummating the destruction of our common enemies. It behoves us public men ever to set an extreme example. Which one can I spare, I wonder?" And he fixed upon a large rambling tooth on the left wing of his lower jaw. "It will hurt horribly, I'm afraid; and if I have an anaesthetic there will be someone else present; and not improbably I shall feel ill afterwards, and be unable to form a clear judgment. I must steel myself. Blink!"

For Blink was making tremulous advances to the teeth. "How pleasant to be a dog!" thought Mr. Lavender, "and know nothing of Germans and teeth. I shall be very unhappy till this is out; but Aurora recommended me, and I must not complain, but rather consider myself the most fortunate of public men." And, ruffling his hair till it stood up all over his head, while his loose eyebrow worked up and down, he gazed at the moon-cat.

"Moon-cat," he said suddenly, "we are but creatures of chance, unable to tell from one day to another what Fate has in store for us. My tooth is beginning to ache already. That is, perhaps, as it should be, for I shall not forget which one it is. "So musing he resumed his teeth; and, going to his bookcase, sought fortitude and inspiration in the records of a Parliamentary debate on enemy aliens.

It was not without considerable trepidation, however, on the following afternoon that he made his way up Welkin Street, and rang at the number on the envelope in his hand.

"Yes sir, doctor is at home," said the maid.

Mr. Lavender's heart was about to fail him when, conjuring up the vision of Aurora, he said in a faint voice: "I wish to see him professionally." And, while the maid departed up the stairs, he waited in the narrow hall, alternately taking his hat off and putting it on again, so great was his spiritual confusion.

"Doctor will see you at once, sir."

Putting his hat on hastily, Mr. Lavender followed her upstairs, feeling at his tooth to make quite sure that he remembered which it was. His courage mounted as he came nearer to his fate, and he marched into the room behind the maid holding his hat on firmly with one hand and his tooth in firmly with the other. There, beside a red velvet dentist's chair, he saw a youngish man dressed in a white coat, with round eyes and a domestic face, who said in good English:

"What can I do for you, my dear sir? I fear you are in bain."

"In great pain," replied Mr. Lavender faintly, "in great pain." And, indeed, he was; for the nervous crisis from which he was suffering had settled in the tooth, on which he still pressed a finger through his cheek.

"Sit down, sir, sit down," said the young man, "and perhaps it would be better if you should remove your hat. We shall not hurd you - no, no, we shall not hurd you."

At those words, which seemed to cast doubt on his courage, Mr. Lavender recovered all his presence of mind. He took off his hat, advanced resolutely to the chair, sat down in it, and, looking up, said:

"Do to me what you will; I shall not flinch, nor depart in any way from the behaviour of those whose duty it is to set an example to others."

So saying, he removed his teeth, and placing them in a bowl on the little swinging table which he perceived on his left hand, he closed his eyes, put his finger in his mouth, and articulated:

"'Ith one."

"Excuse me, sir," said the young German, "but do you wish a dooth oud?"

"'At ish my deshire," said Mr. Lavender, keeping his finger on his tooth, and his eyes closed. "'At one."

"I cannot give you gas without my anaesthedist."

"I dow," said Mr. Lavender; "be wick."

And, feeling the little cold spy-glass begin to touch his gums, he clenched his hands and thought: "This is the moment to prove that I, too, can die for a good cause. If I am not man enough to bear for my country so small a woe I can never again look Aurora in the face."

The voice of the young dentist dragged him rudely from the depth of his resignation.

"Excuse me, but which dooth did you say?"

Mr. Lavender again inserted his finger, and opened his eyes.

The dentist shook his head. "Imbossible," he said; "that dooth is perfectly sound. The other two are rotten. But they do not ache?"

Mr. Lavender shook his head and repeated:

"At one."

"You are my first client this week, sir," said the young German calmly, "but I cannot that dooth dake out."

At those words Mr. Lavender experienced a sensation as if his soul were creeping back up his legs; he spoke as it reached his stomach.

"Noc?" he said.

"No," replied the young German. It is nod the dooth which causes you the bain.

Mr. Lavender, suddenly conscious that he had no pain, took his finger out.

"Sir," he said, "I perceive that you are an honourable man. There is something sublime in your abnegation if, indeed, you have had no other client this week.

"No fear," said the young German. "Haf I, Cicely?"

Mr. Lavender became conscious for the first time of a young woman leaning up against the wall, with a pair of tweezers in her hand.

"Take it out, Otto," she said in a low voice, "if he wants it."

"No no," said Mr. Lavender sharply, resuming his teeth; "I would not for the world burden your conscience."

"My clients are all batriots," said the young dentist, "and my bractice is Kaput. We are in a bad way, sir," he added, with a smile, "but we try to do the correct ting."

Mr. Lavender saw the young woman move the tweezers in a manner which caused his blood to run a little cold.

"We must live," he heard her say.

"Young madam," he said, "I honour the impulse which makes you desire to extend your husband's practice. Indeed, I perceive you both to be so honourable that I cannot but make you a confession. My tooth is indeed sound, though, since I have been pretending that it isn't, it has caused me much discomfort. I came here largely to form an opinion of your husband's character, with a view to securing his internment."

At that word the two young people shrank together till they were standing side by side, staring at Mr Lavender with eyes full of anxiety and wonder. Their hands, which still held the implements of dentistry, insensibly sought each other.

Be under no apprehension," cried Mr. Lavender, much moved; "I can see that you are greatly attached, and even though your husband is a German, he is still a man, and I could never bring myself to separate him from you."

"Who are you?" said the young woman in a frightened voice, putting her arm round her husband's waist.

"Just a public man," answered Mr. Lavender.

"I came here from a sense of duty; nothing more, assure you."

"Who put you up to it?

"That," said Mr. Lavender, bowing as best he could

from the angle he was in, "I am not at liberty to disclose. But, believe me, you have nothing to fear from this visit; I shall never do anything to distress a woman. And please charge me as if the tooth had been extracted."

The young German smiled, and shook his head.

"Sir," he said, "I am grateful to you for coming, for it shows us what danger we are in. The hardest ting to bear has been the uncertainty of our bosition, and the feeling that our friends were working behind our backs. Now we know that this is so we shall vordify our souls to bear the worst. But, tell me," he went on, "when you came here, surely you must have subbosed that to tear me away from my wife would be very bainful to her and to myself. You say now you never could do that, how was it, then, you came?"

"Ah, sir!" cried Mr. Lavender, running his hands through his hair and staring at the ceiling, "I feared this might seem inconsistent to your logical German mind. But there are many things we public men would never do if we could see them being done. Fortunately, as a rule we cannot. Believe me, when I leave you I shall do my best to save you from a fate which I perceive to be unnecessary."

So saying, he rose from the chair, and, picking up his hat, backed towards the door.

"I will not offer you my hand," he said, "for I am acutely conscious that my position is neither dignified nor decent. I owe you a tooth that I shall not readily forget. Good-bye!"

And backing through the doorway he made his way down the stairs and out into the street, still emotionalized by the picture of the two young people holding each other by the waist. He had not, however, gone far before reason resumed its sway, and he began to see that the red velvet chair in which he had been sitting was in reality a wireless apparatus reaching to Berlin, or at least concealed a charge of dynamite to blow up some King or Prime Minister; and that the looking-glasses, of which he had noticed two at least, were surely used for signalling to Gothas or Zeppelins. This plunged him into a confusion so poignant that, rather by accident than design, he found himself again at Hampstead instead of at Scotland Yard. "In the society of Aurora alone," he thought, "can I free myself from the goadings of conscience, for it was she who sent me on that errand." And, instead of going in, he took up a position on his lawn whence he could attract her attention by waving his arms. He had been doing this for some time, to the delight of Blink, who thought it a new game, before he saw her in her nurse's dress coming out of a French-window with her yellow book in her hand. Redoubling his efforts till he had arrested her attention, he went up to the privet hedge, and said, in a deep and melancholy voice:

"Aurora, I have failed in my duty, and the errand on which you sent me is unfulfilled. Mrs. Pullbody's sister's husband's sister's husband is still, largely speaking, at large."

"I knew he would be," replied the young lady, with her joyous smile, "that's why I put her on to you - the cat!"

At a loss to understand her meaning, Mr. Lavender, who had bent forward above the hedge in his eagerness to explain, lost his balance, and, endeavouring to save the hedge, fell over into some geranium pots.

"Dear Don Pickwixote," cried the young lady, assisting him to rise, "have you hurt your nose?"

"It is not that," said Mr. Lavender, removing some mould from his hair, and stifling the attentions of Blink; "but rather my honour, for I have allowed my duty to my country to be overridden by the common emotion of pity."

"Hurrah!" cried the young lady. "It'll do you ever so much good."

"Aurora!" cried Mr. Lavender aghast, walking at her side. But the young lady only uttered her enchanting laugh.

"Come and lie down in the hammock!" she said you're looking like a ghost. I'll cover you up with a rug, and smoke a cigarette to keep the midges off you. Tuck up your legs; that's right!"

"No!" said Mr. Lavender from the recesses of the hammock, feeling his nose, "let the bidges bide me. I deserve they should devour me alive.

"All right," said the young lady. "But have a nap, anyway! "And sitting down in a low chair, she opened her book and lit a cigarette.

Mr. Lavender remained silent, watching her with the eyes of an acolyte, and wondering whether he was in his senses to have alighted on so rare a fortune. Nor was it long before he fell into a hypnotic doze.

How long Mr. Lavender had been asleep he could not of course tell before he dreamed that he was caught in a net, the meshes of which were formed of the cries of newspaper boys announcing atrocities by land and sea. He awoke looking into the eyes of Aurora, who, to still his struggles, had taken hold of his ankles.

"My goodness! You are thin!" were the first words he heard. "No wonder you're lightheaded."

Mr. Lavender, whose returning chivalry struggled with unconscious delight, murmured with difficulty:

"Let me go, let me go; it is too heavenly!

"Well, have you finished kicking?" asked the young lady.

"Yes," returned Mr. Lavender in a fainting voice -- " alas!"

The young lady let go of his ankles, and, aiding him to rise from the hammock, said: "I know what's the matter with you now - you're starving yourself. You ought to be kept on your back for three months at least, and fed on butter."

Mr. Lavender, soothing the feelings of Blink, who, at his struggles, had begun to pant deeply, answered with watering lips:

"Everyone in these days must do twice as much as he ought, and I eat half, for only in this way can we compass the defeat of our common enemies." The young lady's answer, which sounded like "Bosh!" was lost in Mr. Lavender's admiration of her magnificent proportions as she bent to pick up her yellow book.

"Aurora," he said, "I know not what secret you share with the goddesses; suffer me to go in and give thanks for this hour spent in your company."

And he was about to recross the privet hedge when she caught him by the coat-tag, saying:

"No, Don Pickwixote, you must dine with us. I want you to meet my father. Come along!" And, linking her arm in his, she led him towards her castle. Mr. Lavender, who had indeed no, option but to obey, such was the vigour of her arm, went with a sense of joy not unmingled with consternation lest the personage she spoke of should have viewed him in the recent extravagance of his dreaming moments.

"I don't believe," said the young lady, gazing down at him, "that you weigh an ounce more than seven stone. It's appalling!"

"Not," returned Mr. Lavender, "by physical weight and force shall we win this war, for it is at bottom a question of morale. Right is, ever victorious in the end, and though we have infinitely greater material resources than our foes, we should still triumph were we reduced to the last ounce, because of the inherent nobility of our cause."

"You'll be reduced to the last ounce if we don't feed, you up somehow," said the young lady.

"Would you like to wash your hands?"

Mr. Lavender having signified his assent, she left him

alone in a place covered with linoleum. When, at length, followed by Blink, he emerged from dreamy ablutions, Mr. Lavender, saw that she had changed her dress to a flowing blue garment of diaphanous character, which made her appear, like an emanation of the sky. He was about to say so when he noticed a gentleman in khaki scrutinizing him with lively eyes slightly injected with blood.

"Don Pickwixote," said the young lady; "my father, Major Scarlet."

Mr. Lavender's hand was grasped by one which seemed to him made of iron.

"I am honoured, sir," he said painfully, "to meet the father of my charming young neighbour."

The Major answered in a voice as clipped as his grey bottle-brush moustache, "Delighted! Dinner's ready. Come along!"

Mr. Lavender saw that he had a mouth which seemed to have a bitt in it; several hairs on a finely rounded head; and an air of efficient and truculent bonhomie tanned and wrinkled by the weather.

The table at which they became seated seemed to one accustomed to frugality to groan with flowers and china and glass; and Mr. Lavender had hardly supped his rich and steaming soup before his fancy took fire; nor did he notice that he was drinking from a green glass in which was a yellow fluid.

"I get Army rations," said the Major, holding a morsel of fillet of beef towards Blink. "Nice dog,

Mr. Lavender."

"Yes," replied Mr. Lavender, ever delighted that his favourite should receive attention, "she is an angel."

"Too light," said the Major, "and a bit too narrow in front; but a nice dog. What's your view of the war?"

Before Mr. Lavender could reply he felt Aurora's foot pressing his, and heard her say:

"Don Pickwixote's views are after your own heart, Dad; he's for the complete destruction of the Hun."

"Indeed, yes," cried Mr. Lavender with shining eyes. "Right and justice demand it. We seek to gain nothing!"

"But we'll take all we can get," said the Major.

"They'll never get their Colonies back. We'll stick to them fast enough."

Mr. Lavender stared at him for a moment, then, remembering what he had so often read, he murmured:

"Aggrandizement is not our object; but we can never forget that so long as any territory remains in the hands of our treacherous foe the arteries of our far-flung Empire are menaced at the roots."

"Right-o," said the Major, "we've got the chance of our lives, and we're going to take it."

Mr. Lavender sat forward a little on his chair. "I shall never admit," he said, "that we are going to take anything, for that would be contrary to the principles which we are pledged to support, and to our avowed intention of seeking only the benefit of the human race; but our inhuman foes have compelled us to deprive them of the power to injure others."

"Yes," said the Major, "we must just go on killing Germans and collaring every bit of their property we can."

Mr. Lavender sat a little further forward on his chair, and the trouble in his eyes grew.

"After all's said and done," continued the Major; "it's a simple war - us or them! And in the long run it's bound to be us. We've got the cards." Mr. Lavender started, and said in a weak and wavering voice:

"We shall never sheathe the sword until -- "

"The whole bag of tricks is in our hands. Might isn't Right, but Right's Might, Mr. Lavender; ha, ha!"

Mr. Lavender's eyes lighted on his glass, and he emptied it in his confusion. When he looked up again he could not see the Major very well, but could distinctly hear the truculent bonhomie of his voice.

"Every German ought to be interned; all their property ought to be confiscated; all their submarines' and Zeppelins' crews ought to be hung; all German prisoners ought to be treated as they treat our men. We ought to give 'em no quarter. We ought to bomb their towns out of existence. I draw the line at their women. Short of that there's nothing too bad for them. I'd treat ' em like rabbits. Vermin they were, and vermin they remain."

During this speech the most astounding experience befell Mr. Lavender, so that his eyes nearly started from his head. It seemed to him, indeed, that he was seated at dinner with a Prussian, and the Major's voice had no sooner ceased its genial rasping than with a bound forward on his chair, he ejaculated:

"Behold the man - the Prussian in his jack-boot!" And, utterly oblivious of the fact that he was addressing Aurora's father, he went on with almost terrible incoherence: "Although you have conquered this country, sir, never shall you subdue in my breast the sentiments of liberty and generosity which make me an Englishman. I abhor you - invader of the world - trampler underfoot of the humanities - enemy of mankind - apostle of force! You have blown out the sparks of love and kindliness, and have for ever robbed the Universe. Prussian!"

The emphasis with which he spoke that word caused his chair, on the edge of which he was sitting, to tilt up under him so that he slid under the table, losing the vision of that figure in helmet and field-grey which he had been apostrophizing.

"Hold up!" said a voice, while Blink joined him nervously beneath the board.

"Never!" cried Mr. Lavender. "Imprison, maltreat me do what you will. You have subdued her body, but never will I admit that you have conquered the honour of Britain and trodden her gentle culture into the mud."

And, convinced that he would now be dragged away to

be confined in some dungeon on bread and water, he clasped the leg of the dining-table with all his might, while Blink, sagaciously aware that something peculiar was occurring to her master, licked the back of his neck. He had been sitting there perhaps half a minute, with his ears stretched to catch the half-whispered sounds above, when he saw a shining object appear under the table, the head, indeed, of the Prussian squatting there to look at him.

"Go up, thou bald-head," he called out at once; "I will make no terms with the destroyer of justice and humanity."

"All right, my dear sir," replied the head.

"Will you let my daughter speak to you?"

"Prussian blasphemer," responded Mr. Lavender, shifting his position so as to be further away, and clasping instead of the table leg some soft silken objects, which he was too excited to associate with Aurora, "you have no daughter, for no woman would own one whose hated presence poisons this country."

"Well, well," said the Major. "How shall we get him out?"

Hearing these words, and believing them addressed to a Prussian guard, Mr. Lavender clung closer to the objects, but finding them wriggle in his clasp let go, and, bolting forward like a rabbit on his hands and knees, came into contact with the Major's head. The sound of the concussion, the Major's oaths, Mr. Lavender's moans, Blink's barking, and the peals of laughter from Aurora made up a noise which might have been heard in Portugal. The situation was not eased until Mr. Lavender crawled out, and taking up a dinner-knife, rolled his napkin round his arm, and prepared to defend himself against the German Army.

"Well, I'm damned," said the Major when he saw these preparations; "I am damned."

Aurora, who had been leaning against the wall from laughter, here came forward, gasping:

"Go away, Dad, and leave him to me."

"To you!" cried the Major. "He's not safe!"

"Oh yes, he is; it's only you that are exciting him. Come along!"

And taking her father by the arm she conducted him from the room. Closing the door behind him, and putting her back against it, she said, gently:

"Dear Don Pickwixote, all danger is past. The enemy has been repulsed, and we are alone in safety. Ha, ha, ha!"

Her voice recalled. Mr. Lavender from his strange hallucination. "What?" he said weakly.

"Why? Who? Where? When?"

"You have been dreaming again. Let me take you home, and tuck you into bed." And taking from him the knife and napkin, she opened the French-window, and passed out on to the lawn.

Lavender, who now that his reason had come back, would have followed her to the death, passed out also, accompanied by Blink, and watched by the Major, who had put his head in again at the door. Unfortunately, the spirit moved Mr. Lavender to turn round at this moment, and seeing the head he cried out in a loud voice:

"He is there! He is there! Arch enemy of mankind! Let me go and die under his jackboot, for never over my living body shall he rule this land." And the infatuated gentleman would certainly have rushed at his host had not Aurora stayed him by the slack of his nether garments. The Major withdrawing his head, Mr. Lavender's excitement again passed from him, and he suffered himself to be led dazedly away and committed to the charge of Mrs. Petty and Joe, who did not leave him till he was in bed with a strong bromide to keep him company.

XVI

FIGHTS THE FIGHT OF FAITH

The strenuous experiences through which Mr. Lavender had passed resulted in what Joe Petty called "a fair knock-out," and he was forced to spend three days in the seclusion of his bed, deprived of his newspapers. He instructed Mrs. Petty, however, on no account to destroy or mislay any journal, but to keep them in a pile in his study. This she did, for though her first impulse was to light the kitchen fire with the five of them every morning, deliberate reflection convinced her that twenty journals read at one sitting would produce on him a more soporific effect than if he came down to a mere five.

Mr. Lavender passed his three days, therefore, in perfect repose, feeding Blink, staring at the ceiling, and conversing with Joe. An uneasy sense that he had been lacking in restraint caused his mind to dwell on life as seen by the monthly rather than the daily papers, and to hold with his chauffeur discussions of a somewhat philosophical character.

"As regards the government of this country, Joe," he said, on the last evening of his retirement, "who do you consider really rules? For it is largely on this that our future must depend."

"Can't say, sir," answered Joe, "unless it's Botty."

"I do not know whom or what you signify by that word," replied Mr. Lavender; "I am wondering if it is the People who rule."

"The People!" replied Joe;" the People's like a gent in a lunatic asylum, allowed to 'ave instinks but not to express 'em. One day it'll get aht, and we shall all step lively."

"It is, perhaps, Public Opinion," continued Mr. Lavender to himself, "as expressed in the Press."

"Not it," said Joe the nearest opinion the Press gets to expressin' is that of Mayors. 'Ave you never noticed, sir, that when the Press is 'ard up for support of an opinion that the public don't 'old, they go to the Mayors, and get 'em in two columns?"

"Mayors are most valuable public men," said Mr. Lavender.

"I've nothin' against 'em," replied Joe; "very average lot in their walk of life; but they ain't the People."

Mr. Lavender sighed. "What, then, is the People, Joe?"

"I am," replied Joe; "I've got no opinions on anything except that I want to live a quiet life - just enough beer and 'baccy, short hours, and no worry."

"'If you compare that with the aspirations of Mayors you will see how sordid such a standard is," said Mr. Lavender, gravely.

"Sordid it may be, sir," replied Joe; "but there's, a thing abaht it you 'aven't noticed. I don't want to sacrifice nobody to satisfy my aspirations. Why? Because I've got none. That's priceless. Take the Press, take Parlyment, take Mayors - all mad on aspirations. Now it's Free Trade, now it's Imperialism; now it's Liberty in Europe; now it's Slavery in Ireland; now it's sacrifice of the last man an' the last dollar. You never can tell what aspiration'll get 'em next. And the 'ole point of an aspiration is the sacrifice of someone else. Don't you make a mistake, sir. I defy you to make a public speech which 'asn't got that at the bottom of it."

"We are wandering from the point, Joe," returned Mr. Lavender. "Who is it that governs, the country?"

"A Unseen Power," replied Joe promptly.

"How?"

"Well, sir, we're a democratic country, ain't we? Parlyment's elected by the People, and Gover'ment's elected by Parlyment. All right so far; but what 'appens? Gover'ment says 'I'm going to do this.' So long as it meets with the approval of the Unseen Power, well an' good. But what if it don't? The U.P. gets busy; in an 'undred papers there begins to appear what the U.P. calls Public Opinion, that's to say the opinion of the people that agree with the U.P. There you 'ave it, sir, only them - and it appears strong. Attacks on the Gover'ment policy, nasty things said abaht members of it that's indiscreet enough to speak aht what, they think - German fathers, and other secret vices; an' what's more than all, not a peep at any opinion that supports the Gover'ment. Well, that goes on day after day, playin' on the mind of Parlyment, if they've got any, and gittin' on the Gover'ment's nerves, which they've got weak, till they says: 'Look 'ere, it's no go; Public Opinion won't stand it. We shall be outed; and that'll never do, because there's no other set of fellows that can save this country.' Then they 'ave a meetin' and change their policy. And what they've never seen is that they've never seen Public Opinion at all. All they've seen is what the U.P. let 'em. Now if I was the Gover'ment, I'd 'ave it out once for all with the U. P."

"Ah!" cried Mr. Lavender, whose eyes were starting from his, head, so profoundly was he agitated by what was to him a new thought.

"Yes," continued Joe, "if I was the Gover'ment, next time it 'appened, I'd say: 'All right, old cock, do your damnedest. I ain't responsible to you. Attack, suppress, and all the rest of it. We're goin' to do what we say, all the same!' And then I'd do it. And what'd come of it? Either the U.P. would go beyond the limits of the Law - and then I'd jump on it, suppress its papers, and clap it into quod - or it'd take it lyin' down. Whichever 'appened it'd be all up with the U. P. I'd a broke its chain off my neck for good. But I ain't the Gover'ment, an Gover'ment's got tender feet. I ask you, sir, wot's the good of havin' a Constitooshion, and a the bother of electing these fellows, if they can't act according to their judgment for the short term of their natural lives? The U.P. may be patriotic and estimable, and 'ave the best intentions and all that, but its outside the Constitooshion; and what's more, I'm not goin' to spend my last blood an' my last money in a democratic country to suit the tastes of any single man, or triumpherate, or wotever it may be made of. If the Government's uncertain wot the country wants they can always ask it in the proper way, but they never ought to take it on 'earsay from the papers. That's wot I think."

While he was speaking Mr. Lavender had become excited to the point of fever, for, without intending it, Joe had laid bare to him a yawning chasm between his worship of public men and his devotion to the Press. And no sooner had his chauffeur finished than he cried: "Leave me, Joe, for I must think this out."

"Right, sir," answered Joe with his smile, and taking the tea-tray from off his master, he set it where it must infallibly be knocked over, and went out.

"Can it be possible," thought Mr. Lavender, when he was alone, "that I am serving God and Mammon? And which is God and which is Mammon?" he added, letting his thoughts play over the countless speeches and leading articles which had formed his spiritual diet since the war began. "Or, indeed, are they not both God or both Mammon? If what Joe says is true, and nothing is recorded save what seems good to this Unseen Power, have I not been listening to ghosts and shadows; and am I, indeed, myself anything but the unsubstantial image of a public man? For it is true that I have no knowledge of anything save what is recorded in the papers." And perceiving that the very basis of his faith was endangered, he threw off the bedclothes, and began to pace the room. "Are we, then, all," he thought, "being bounded like india-rubber balls by an unseen hand; and is there no one of us strong enough to bounce into the eye of our bounder and overthrow him? My God, I am unhappy; for it is a terrible thing not to know which my God is, and whether I am a public man or an india-rubber ball. "And the more he thought the more dreadful it seemed to him, now that he perceived that all those journals, pamphlets, and reports with which his study walls were lined might not be the truth, but merely authorized versions of it.

"This," he said aloud, "is a nightmare from which I must awaken or lose all my power of action and my ability to help my country in its peril."

And sudden sweat broke out on his brow, for he perceived that he had now no means of telling even whether there was a peril, so strangely had Joe's words affected his powers of credulity.

"But surely," he thought, steadying himself by gripping his washstand, "there was, at least, a peril once. And yet, how do I know even that, for I have only been told so; and the tellers themselves were only told so by this Unseen Power; and suppose it has made a mistake or has some private ends to serve! Oh! it is terrible, and there is no end to it. "And he shook the crockery in the spasms which followed the first awakenings of these religious doubts. "Where, then, am I to go," he cried, "for knowledge of the truth? For even books would seem dependent on the good opinion of this Unseen Power, and would not reach my eyes unless they were well spoken of by it."

And the more he thought the more it seemed to him that nothing could help him but to look into the eyes of this Unseen Power, so that he might see for himself whether it was the Angel of Truth or some Demon jumping on the earth. No sooner had this conviction entered his brain than he perceived how in carrying out such an enterprise he would not only be setting his own mind at rest, and re-establishing or abolishing his faith, but would be doing the greatest service which he could render to his country and to all public men. "Thus," he thought, "shall I cannonize my tourney, and serve Aurora, who is the dawn of truth and beauty in the world. I am not yet worthy, however, of this adventure, which will, indeed, be far more arduous and distressing to accomplish than any which I have yet undertaken. What can I do to brighten and equip my mind and divest it of all those prejudices in which it may unconsciously have become steeped? If I could leave the earth a short space and commune with the clouds it might be best. I will go to Hendon and see if someone will take me up for a consideration; for on earth I can no longer be sure of anything."

And having rounded off his purpose with this lofty design, he went back to bed with his head lighter than a puff-ball.

XVII

ADDRESSES THE CLOUDS

On the morning following his resurrection Mr. Lavender set out very early for the celebrated flying ground without speaking of his intention to anyone. At the bottom of the hill he found to his annoyance that Blink had divined his purpose and was following. This, which compelled him to walk, greatly delayed his arrival. But chance now favoured him, for he found he was expected, and at once conducted to a machine which was about to rise. A taciturn young man, with a long jaw, and wings on his breast, was standing there gazing at it with an introspective eye.

"Ready, sir?" he said.

"Yes," replied Mr. Lavender, enveloped to the eyes in a garment of fur and leather. "Will you kindly hold my dog?" he added, stroking Blink with the feeling that he was parting for ever with all that was most dear to him.

An attendant having taken hold of her by the collar, Mr. Lavender was heaved into the machine, where the young airman was already seated in front of him.

"Shall I feel sick?" asked Mr. Lavender.

"Probably," said the young airman.

"That will not deter me, for the less material I become the better it will be."

The young airman turned his head, and Mr. Lavender caught the surprised yellow of his eye.

"Hold on," said the airman, "I'm going to touch her off."

Mr. Lavender held on, and the machine moved but at this moment Blink, uttering a dismal howl, leapt forward, and, breaking from the attendant's grasp, landed in the machine against Mr. Lavender's chest.

"Stop! stop he cried!" my dog.

"Stuff her down," said the unmoved airman, "between your legs. She's not the first to go up and won't be the last to come down."

Mr. Lavender stuffed her down as best he could. "If we are to be killed," he thought, "it will be together. Blink!" The faithful creature, who bitterly regretted her position now that the motion had begun, looked up with a darkened eye at Mr. Lavender, who was stopping his ears against the horrible noises which had now begun. He too, had become aware of the pit of his stomach; but this sensation soon passed away in the excitement he felt at getting away from the earth, for they were already at the height of a house, and rising rapidly.

"It is not at all like a little bird," he thought, but rather resembles a slow train on the surface of the sea, or a horse on a switchback merry-go-round. I feel, however, that my spirit will soon be free, for the earth is becoming like a board whereon a game is played by an unseen hand, and I am leaving it." And craning his head out a little too far he felt his chin knock against his spine. Drawing it in with difficulty he concentrated his attention upon that purification of his spirit which was the object of his journey.

"I am now," he thought, "in the transcendent ether. It should give me an amazing power of expression such as only the greatest writers and orators attain; and, divorced as I am rapidly becoming from all sordid reality, truth will appear to me like one of those stars towards which I am undoubtedly flying though I cannot as yet see it."

Blink, who between his legs had hitherto been unconscious of their departure from the earth, now squirmed irresistibly up till her forepaws were on her master's chest, and gazed lugubriously at the fearful prospect. Mr. Lavender clasped her convulsively. They were by now rapidly nearing a flock of heavenly sheep, which as they approached became ever more gigantic till they were transformed into monstrous snow-fleeces intersected by wide drifts of blue.

"Can it be that we are to adventure above them?" thought Mr. Lavender. "I hope not, for they seem to me fearful." His alarm was soon appeased, for the machine began to take a level course a thousand feet, perhaps, below the clouds, whence little wraiths wandering out now and again dimmed Mr. Lavender's vision and moistened his brow.

Blink having retired again between her master's legs, a

sense of security and exaltation was succeeding to the natural trepidation of Mr. Lavender's mood. "I am now," he thought, "lifted above all petty plots and passions on the wings of the morning. Soon will great thoughts begin to jostle in my head, and I shall see the truth of all things made clear at last."

But the thoughts did not jostle, a curious lethargy began stealing over him instead, so that his head fell back, and his mouth fell open. This might have endured until he returned to earth had not the airman stopped the engines so that they drifted ruminantly in space below the clouds. With the cessation of the noise Mr. Lavender's brain regained its activity, and he was enchanted to hear the voice of his pilot saying:

"How are you getting on, sir?"

"As regards the sensation," Mr. Lavender replied, "it is marvellous, for after the first minute or two, during which the unwonted motion causes a certain inconvenience, one grasps at once the exhilaration and joy of this great adventure. To be in motion towards the spheres, and see the earth laid out like a chess-board below you; to feel the lithe creature beneath your body responding so freely to every call of its gallant young pilot; to be filled with the scream of the engines, as of an eagle at sport; to know that at the least aberration of the intrepid airman we should be dashed into a million pieces; all this is largely to experience an experience so unforgettable that one will never - er - er - forget it."

"Gosh!" said the young airman.

"Yes," pursued Mr. Lavender, who was now unconsciously reading himself in his morning's paper, "one can only compare the emotion to that which the disembodied spirit might feel passing straight from earth to heaven. We saw at a great depth below us on a narrow white riband of road two crawling black specks, and knew that they were human beings, the same and no more than we had been before we left that great common place called Earth."

"Gum!" said the young airman, as Lavender paused, "you're getting it fine, sir! Where will it appear?"

"Those great fleecy beings the clouds," went on Mr. Lavender, without taking on the interruption, "seemed to await our coming in the morning glory of their piled-up snows; and we, with the rarefied air in our lungs, felt that we must shout to them." And so carried away was Mr. Lavender by his own style that he really did begin to address the clouds: "Ghosts of the sky, who creep cold about this wide blue air, we small adventuring mortals great-hearted salute you. Humbly proud of our daring have we come to sport with you and the winds of Ouranos, and, in the rapturous corridors between you, play hide-and seek, avoiding your glorious moisture with the dips and curves and skimming of our swallow flights - we, the little unconquerable Spirits of the Squirth!"

The surprise which Mr. Lavender felt at having uttered so peculiar a word, in the middle of such a flow of poetry reduced him to sudden silence.

"Golly!" said the airman with sudden alarm in his voice. "Hold tight!" And they began to shoot towards earth faster than they had risen. They came down, by what seemed a miracle to Mr. Lavender, who was still contemplative, precisely where they had gone up. A little group was collected there, and as they stepped out a voice said, "I beg your pardon," in a tone so dry that it pierced even the fogged condition in which Mr. Lavender alighted. The gentleman who spoke had a dark moustache and thick white hair, and, except that he wore a monocle, and was perhaps three inches taller, bore a striking resemblance to himself.

"Thank you," he replied, "certainly."

"No," said the gentleman, "not at all - on the contrary, Who the hell are you?"

"A public man," said Mr. Lavender, surprised; "at least," he added conscientiously, "I am not quite certain."

"Well," said the gentleman, "you've jolly well stolen my stunt."

"Who, then, are you?" asked Mr. Lavender.

"I?" replied the gentleman, evidently intensely surprised that he was not known; "I - my name -- "

But at this moment Mr. Lavender's attention was diverted by the sight of Blink making for the horizon, and crying out in a loud voice: "My dog!" he dropped the coat in which he was still enveloped and set off running after her at full speed, without having taken in the identity of the gentleman or disclosed his own. Blink, indeed, scenting another flight in the air, had made straight for the entrance of the enclosure, and finding a motor cab there with the door open had bolted into it, taking it for her master's car. Mr. Lavender sprang in after her. At the shake which this imparted to the cab, the driver, who had been dozing, turned his head.

"Want to go back, sir?" he said.

"Yes," replied Mr. Lavender, breathless; "London."

XVIII

SEES TRUTH FACE TO FACE

"I fear," thought Mr. Lavender, as they sped towards Town, "that I have inadvertently taken a joy-ride which belonged to that distinguished person with the eyeglass. No matter, my spirit is now bright for the adventure I have in hand. If only I knew where I could find the Unseen Power - but possibly its movements may be recorded in these journals. "And taking from his pocket his morning papers, which he had not yet had time to peruse, he buried himself in their contents. He was still deeply absorbed when the cab stopped and the driver knocked on the window. Mr. Lavender got out, followed by Blink, and was feeling in his pocket for the fare when an exclamation broke from the driver:

"Gorblimy! I've brought the wrong baby!"

And before Mr. Lavender had recovered from his surprise, he had whipped the car round and was speeding back towards the flying ground.

"How awkward!" thought Mr. Lavender, who was extremely nice in money matters; "what shall I do now?" And he looked around him. There, as it were by a miracle, was the office of a great journal, whence obviously his distinguished colleague had set forth to the flying grounds, and to which he had been returned in error by the faithful driver.

Perceiving in all this the finger of Providence, Mr. Lavender walked in. Those who have followed his experiences so far will readily understand how no one could look on Mr. Lavender without perceiving him to be a man of extreme mark, and no surprise need be felt when he was informed that the Personage he sought was on the point of visiting Brighton to open a hospital, and might yet be overtaken at Victoria Station.

With a beating heart he took up the trail in another taxi-cab, and, arriving at Victoria, purchased tickets for himself and Blink, and inquired for the Brighton train.

"Hurry up!" replied the official. Mr. Lavender ran, searching the carriage windows for any indication of his objective. The whistle had been blown, and he was in despair, when his eye caught the label "Reserved" on a first-class window, and looking in he saw a single person evidently of the highest consequence smoking a cigar, surrounded by papers. Without a moment's hesitation he opened the door, and, preceded by Blink, leaped in. "This carriage is reserved, sir," said the Personage, as the train moved out.

"I know," said Mr. Lavender, who had fallen on to the edge of the seat opposite; "and only the urgency of my business would have caused me to violate the sanctity of your retreat, for, believe me, I have the instincts if not the habits of a gentleman."

The Personage, who had made a move of his hand as if

to bring the train to a standstill, abandoning his design, replaced his cigar, and contemplated Mr. Lavender from above it.

The latter remained silent, returning that remarkable stare, while Blink withdrew beneath the seat and pressed her chin to the ground, savouring the sensation of a new motion.

"Yes," he thought, "those eyes have an almost superhuman force and cunning. They are the eyes of a spider in the centre of a great web. They seem to draw me."

"You are undoubtedly the Unseen Power, sir," he said suddenly, "and I have reached the heart of the mystery. From your own lips I shall soon know whether I am a puppet or a public man."

The Personage, who by his movements was clearly under the impression that he had to do with a lunatic, sat forward with his hands on his knees ready to rise at a moment's notice; he kept his cigar in his mouth, however, and an enforced smile on the folds of his face.

"What can I do for you, sir?" he said.

"Will you have a cigar?"

"No, thank you," replied Mr. Lavender, "I must keep the eyes of my spirit clear, and come to the point. Do you rule this country or do you not? For it is largely on the answer to this that my future depends. In telling others what to do am I speaking as my conscience or as your conscience dictates; and, further, if indeed I am speaking as your conscience dictates, have you a conscience?"

The Personage, who had evidently made up his mind to humour the intruder, flipped the ash off his cigar.

Well, sir, he said, I don't know who the devil you may be, but my conscience is certainly as good as yours."

"That," returned Mr: Lavender with a sigh, is a great relief, for whether you rule the country or not, you are undoubtedly the source from which I, together with the majority of my countrymen, derive our inspirations. You are the fountainhead at which we draw and drink. And to know that your waters are pure, unstained by taint of personal prejudice and the love of power, will fortify us considerably. Am I to assume, then, that above all passion and pettiness, you are an impersonal force whose innumerable daily editions reflect nothing but abstract truth, and are in no way the servants of a preconceived and personal view of the situation?"

"You want to know too much, don't you think?" said the Personage with a smile.

"How can that be, sir?" asked Mr. Lavender: If you are indeed the invisible king swaying the currents of national life, and turning its tides at will, it is essential that we should believe in you; and before we can believe in you must we not know all about you?"

"By Jove, sir," replied the Personage, "that strikes me as being contrary to all the rules of religion. I thought faith was the ticket."

By this answer Mr. Lavender was so impressed that he sat for a moment in silence, with his eyebrow working up and down.

"Sir," he said at last, "you have given me a new thought. If you are right, to disbelieve in you and the acts which you perform, or rather the editions which you issue, is blasphemy."

"I should think so," said the Personage, emitting a long whiff of smoke. Hadn't that ever occurred to you before?"

"No," replied Mr. Lavender, naively, "for I have never yet disbelieved anything in those journals."

The Personage coughed heartily.

"I have always regarded them," went on Mr. Lavender, "as I myself should wish to be regarded, 'without fear and without reproach.' For that is, as I understand it, the principle on which a gentleman must live, ever believing of others what he would wish believed of himself. With the exception of Germans," he added hastily.

"Naturally," returned the Personage. "And I'll defy you to find anything in them which disagrees with that formula. Everything they print refers to Germans if not directly then obliquely. Germans are the 'idee fixe', and without an 'idee fixe', as you know, there's no such thing as religion. Do you get me?"

"Yes, indeed," cried Mr. Lavender, enthused, for the whole matter now seemed to him to fall into coherence, and, what was more, to coincide with his preconceptions, so that he had no longer any doubts. "You, sir - the Unseen Power - are but the crystallized embodiment of the national sentiment in time of war; in serving you, and fulfilling the ideas which you concrete in your journals, we public men are servants of the general animus, which in its turn serves the blind and burning instinct of justice. This is eminently satisfactory to me, who would wish no better fate than to be a humble lackey in that house." He had no sooner, however, spoken those words than Joe Petty's remarks about Public Opinion came back to him, and he added: "But are you really the general animus, or are you only the animus of Mayors, that is the question?"

The personage seemed to follow this thought with difficulty. "What's that?" he said.

Mr. Lavender ran his hands through his hair.

"And turns," he said, "on what is the unit of national feeling and intelligence? Is it or is it not a Mayor?"

The Personage smiled. "Well, what do you think?" he said. "Haven't you ever heard them after dinner? There's no question about it. Make your mind easy if that's your only trouble."

Mr. Lavender, greatly cheered by the genial certainty in this answer, said: "I thank you, sir. I shall go back and refute that common scoffer, that caster of doubts. I have seen the Truth face, to face, and am greatly encouraged to further public effort. With many apologies I can now get out," he added, as the train stopped at South Croydon. "Blink!" And, followed by his dog, he stepped from the train.

The Personage, who was indeed no other than the

private secretary of the private secretary of It whom Mr. Lavender had designated as the Truth watched him from the window.

"Well, that WAS a treat, dear papa!" he murmured to himself, emitting a sigh of smoke after his retreating interlocutor.

XIX

IS IN PERIL OF THE STREET

On the Sunday following this interview with the Truth Mr. Lavender, who ever found the day of rest irksome to his strenuous spirit, left his house after an early supper. It, had been raining all day, but the sinking sun had now emerged and struck its level light into the tree tops from a still cloudy distance. Followed by Blink, he threaded the puddled waste which lies to the west of the Spaniard's Road, nor was it long before the wild beauty of the scene infected his spirit, and he stood still to admire the world spread out. The smoke rack of misted rain was still drifting above the sunset radiance in an apple-green sky; and behind Mr. Lavender, as he gazed at those clouds symbolical of the world's unrest, a group of tall, dark pine-trees, wild and witch-like, had collected as if in audience of his cosmic mood. He formed a striking group for a painter, with the west wind flinging back his white hair, and fluttering his dark moustache along his cheeks, while Blink, a little in front of him, pointed at the prospect and emitted barks whose vigour tossed her charming head now to this side now to that.

"How beautiful is this earth!" thought Mr. Lavender, "and how simple to be good and happy thereon. Yet must we journey ten leagues beyond the wide world's end to find justice and liberty. There are dark powers like lions ever in the path. Yes," he continued, turning round to the pinetrees, who were creaking slightly in the wind, "hate and oppression, greed, lust, and ambition! There you stand malevolently regarding me. Out upon you, dark witches of evil! If I had but an axe I would lay you lower than the dust." But the poor pine-trees paid no attention save to creak a little louder. And so incensed was Mr. Lavender by this insensibility on the part of those which his own words had made him perceive were the powers of darkness that he would very likely have barked his knuckles on them if Blink by her impatience had not induced him to resume his walk and mount on to the noble rampart of the Spaniard's Road.

Along this he wandered and down the hill with the countless ghosts and shadows of his brain, liberating the world in fancy from all the hindrances which beset the paths of public men, till dark fell, and he was compelled to turn towards home. Closely attended by the now sobered Blink he had reached the Tube Station when he perceived in the inky war-time dusk that a woman was following him. Dimly aware that she was tall and graceful he hurried to avoid her, but before long could but note that she was walking parallel and turning her face towards him. Her gloved hand seemed to make a beckoning movement, and perceiving at once that he was the object of that predatory instinct which he knew from the many letters and protests in his journals to be one of the most distressing features of the War, he would have broken into a run if he had not been travelling up-hill; being deprived of this means of escape, his public nature prevailed, and he saw that it was his duty to confront the woman, and strike a blow at, the national evil stalking beside him.

But he was in a difficulty, for his natural delicacy towards women seemed to preclude him from treating her as if she were what she evidently was, while his sense of duty - urged him with equal force to do so.

A whiff of delicious scent determined him. "Madam," he said, without looking in her face, which, indeed, was not visible - so great was the darkness, "it is useless to pursue one who not only has the greatest veneration for women but regards you as a public danger at a time when all the energies of the country should be devoted to the defeat of our common enemies."

The woman, uttering a sound like a laugh, edged towards him, and Mr. Lavender edged away, so that they proceeded up the street crabwise, with Blink adhering jealously to her master's heels.

"Do you know," said Mr. Lavender, with all the delicacy in his power, "how terribly subversive of the national effort it is to employ your beauty and your grace to snare and slacken the sinews of our glorious youth? The mystery of a woman's glance in times like these should be used solely to beckon our heroes on to death in the field. But you, madam, than whom no one indeed has a more mysterious glance, have turned it to ends which, in the words of a great public man, profane the temple of our - our -- "

Mr. Lavender stopped, for his delicacy would not allow him even in so vital a cause to call bodies bodies. The woman here edged so close that he bolted across her in affright, and began to slant back towards the opposite side of the street.

"Madam," he said, you must have perceived by now that I am, alas! not privileged by age to be one of the defenders of my country; and though I am prepared to yield to you, if by so doing I can save some young hero from his fate, I wish you to clearly understand that only my sense of duty as a public man would induce me to do any such thing." At this he turned his eyes dreadfully upon her graceful form still sidling towards him, and, conscious again of that delightful scent, felt a swooning sensation which made him lean against a lamp-post. "Spare me, madam," he said in a faint voice for my country's sake I am ready to do anything, but I must tell you that I worship another of your sex from afar, and if you are a woman you will not seek to make me besmirch that adoration or imperil my chivalry."

So saying, he threw his arms round the lamppost and closed his eyes, expecting every moment to be drawn away against his will into a life of vice.

A well-known voice, strangled to the pitch almost of inaudibility, said in his ear:

"Oh, Don Pickwixote, Don Pickwixote, you will be the death of me!"

Electrified, Mr. Lavender opened his eyes, and in the dull orange rays of the heavily shaded lamp he saw beside him no other than the writhing, choking figure of Aurora herself. Shocked beyond measure by the mistake he had made, Mr. Lavender threw up his hands and bolted past her through the gateway of his garden; nor did he cease running till he had reached his bedroom and got under the bed, so terribly was he upset. There, in the company of Blink, he spent perhaps the most shame-stricken hours of his existence, cursing the memory of all those bishops and novelists who had caused him to believe that every woman in a dark street was a danger to the State; nor could the persuasion of Mrs. Petty or Joe induce him to come out, so that in despair they were compelled to leave him to pass the night in this penitential position, which he did without even taking out his teeth.

XX

RECEIVES A REVELATION

Fully a week elapsed before Mr. Lavender recovered from the effects of the night which he had spent under his bed and again took his normal interest in the course of national affairs. That which at length tore him from his torpid condition and refixed his imagination was an article in one of, his journals on the League of Nations, which caused him suddenly to perceive that this was the most important subject of the day. Carefully extracting the address of the society who had the matter in hand, he determined to go down forthwith and learn from their own lips how he could best induce everybody to join them in their noble undertaking. Shutting every window, therefore and locking Blink carefully into his study, he set forth and took the Tube to Charing Cross.

Arriving at the premises indicated he made his way in lifts and corridors till he came to the name of this great world undertaking upon the door of Room 443, and paused for a moment to recover from the astonishment he felt that the whole building at least was not occupied by the energies of such a prodigious association.

"Appearances, however, are deceptive," he thought;

"and from a single grain of mustard-seed whole fields will flower." He knocked on the door, therefore, and receiving the reply, "Cub id," in a female voice, he entered a room where two young ladies with bad colds were feebly tapping type-writers.

"Can I see the President?" asked Mr. Lavender.

"Dot at the bobent," said one of the young ladies. "Will the Secretary do?"

"Yes," replied Mr. Lavender "for I seek information."

The young ladies indulged in secret confabulation, from which the perpetual word "He" alone escaped to Mr. Lavender's ears.

Then one of them slipped into an inner room, leaving behind her a powerful trail of eucalyptus. She came back almost directly, saying, "Go id."

The room which Mr Lavender entered contained two persons, one seated at a bureau and the other pacing up and down and talking in a powerful bass voice. He paused, looked at Mr. Lavender from under bushy brows, and at once went on walking and talking, with a sort of added zest.

"This must be He," thought Mr. Lavender, sitting down to listen, for there was something about the gentleman which impressed him at once. He had very large red ears, and hardly a hair on his head, while his full, bearded face and prominent eyes were full of force and genius.

"It won't do a little bit, Titmarsh," he was saying, "to

allow the politicians to meddle in this racket. We want men of genius, whose imaginations carry them beyond the facts of the moment. This is too big a thing for those blasted politicians. They haven't shown a sign so far of paying attention to what I've been telling them all this time. We must keep them out, Titmarsh. Machinery without mechanism, and a change of heart in the world. It's very simple. A single man of genius from each country, no pettifogging opposition, no petty prejudices."

The other gentleman, whom Mr. Lavender took for the Secretary, and who was leaning his head rather wearily on his hand, interjected: "Quite so! And whom would you choose besides yourself? In France, for instance?"

He who was walking stopped a moment, again looked at Mr. Lavender intently, and again began to speak as if he were not there.

"France?" he said. "There isn't anybody - Anatole's too old - there isn't anybody."

"America, then?" hazarded the Secretary.

"America!" replied the other; "they haven't got even half a man. There's that fellow in Germany that I used to influence; but I don't know - no, I don't think he'd be any good."

"D'Annunzio, surely -- " began the Secretary.

"D'Annunzio? My God! D'Annunzio! No! There's nobody in Italy or Holland - she's as bankrupt as Spain; and there's not a cat in Austria. Russia might, perhaps, give us someone, but I can't at the moment think of him. No, Titmarsh, it's difficult."

Mr. Lavender had been growing more and more excited at each word he overheard, for a scheme of really stupendous proportions was shaping itself within him. He suddenly rose, and said: "I have an idea."

The Secretary sat up as if he had received a Faradic shock, and he who was walking up and down stood still. "The deuce you have, sir," he said.

"Yes," cried Mr. Lavender and in concentration and marvellous simplicity, "it has, I am sure, never been surpassed. It is clear to me, sir, that you, and you alone, must be this League of Nations. For if it is entirely in your hands there will be no delay. The plan will spring full fledged from the head of Jove, and this great and beneficial change in the lot of mankind will at once become an accomplished fact. There will be no need for keeping in touch with human nature, no call for patience and all that laborious upbuilding stone by stone which is so apt to discourage mankind and imperil the fruition of great reforms. No, sir; you - you must be this League, and we will all work to the end that tomorrow at latest there may be perfected this crowning achievement of the human species."

The gentleman, who had commenced to walk again, looked furtively from Mr. Lavender to the Secretary, and said:

"By Jingo! some idea!"

"Yes," cried Mr. Lavender, entranced that his grand notion should be at once accepted; "for it is only men like you who can both soaringly conceive and immediately concrete in action; and, what is more, there will be no fear of your tiring of this job and taking up another, for you will be IT; and one cannot change oneself."

The gentleman looked at Mr. Lavender very suddenly at the words "tiring of this job," and transferred his gaze to the Secretary, who had bent his face down to his papers, and was smothering a snigger with his hand.

"Who are you, sir?" he said sharply.

"Merely one," returned Mr. Lavender, "who wishes to do all in his power to forward a project so fraught with beneficence to all mankind. I count myself fortunate beyond measure to have come here this morning and found the very Heart of the matter, the grain of mustard-seed."

The gentleman, who had begun to walk again, here muttered words which would have sounded like "Damned impudence" if Mr. Lavender had not been too utterly carried away by his idea to hear them.

"I shall go forth at once," he said, "and make known the good tidings that the fields are sown, the League formed. Henceforth there are no barriers between nations, and the reign of perpetual Peace is assured. It is colossal."

The gentleman abruptly raised his boot, but, seeming to think better of it, lowered it again, and turned away to the window.

Mr. Lavender, having bowed to his back, went out,

and, urged on by his enthusiasm, directed his steps at once towards Trafalgar Square.

Arriving at this hub of the universe he saw that Chance was on his side, for a meeting was already in progress, and a crowd of some forty persons assembled round one of the lions. Owing to his appearance Mr. Lavender was able without opposition to climb up on the plinth and join the speaker, a woman of uncertain years. He stood there awaiting his turn and preparing his oration, while she continued her discourse, which seemed to be a protest against any interference with British control of the freedom of the seas. A Union Jack happened to be leaning against the monument, and when she had at last finished, Mr. Lavender seized it and came forward to the edge.

"Great tidings!" he said at once, waving the flag, and without more ado plunged into an oration, which, so far as it went, must certainly be ranked among his masterpieces. "Great tidings, Friends! I have planted the grain of mustard seed or, in common parlance, have just come from the meeting which has incepted the League of Nations; and it will be my task this morning briefly to make known to you the principles which in future must dominate the policy of the world. Since it is for the closer brotherhood of man and the reign of perpetual peace that we are struggling, we must first secure the annihilation of our common enemies. Those members of the human race whose infamies have largely placed them beyond the pale must be eliminated once for all."

Loud cheers greeted this utterance, and stimulated by the sound Mr. Lavender proceeded: "What, however, must the civilized nations do when at last they have clean sheets? In the first place, all petty prejudices and provincial aspirations must be set aside; and though the world must be firmly founded upon the principle of nationality it must also act as one great people. This, my fellow-countrymen, is no mere contradiction in terms, for though in their new solidarities each nation will be prouder of itself, and more jealous of its good name and independence than ever, that will not prevent its' sacrificing its inalienable rights for the good of the whole human nation of which it is a member. Friends, let me give you a simple illustration, which in a nutshell will make the whole thing clear. We, here in Britain, are justly proud and tenacious of our sea power - in the words of the poet, 'We hold all the gates of the water.' Now it is abundantly and convincingly plain that this reinforced principle of nationality bids us to retain and increase them, while internationalism bids us give - them up."

His audience - which had hitherto listened with open mouths, here closed them, and a strident voice exclaimed:

"Give it a name, gov'nor. D'you say we ought to give up Gib?"

This word pierced Mr. Lavender, standing where he was, to the very marrow, and he fell into such confusion of spirit that his words became inaudible.

"My God!" he thought, appalled; "is it possible that I have not got to the bottom of this question?" And, turning his back on the audience, he gazed in a sort of agony at the figure of Nelson towering into the sky above him. He was about to cry out piteously: "Countrymen, I know not what I think. Oh! I am unhappy!" when he inadvertently stepped back over the edge of the plinth, and, still entangled in the flag, was picked up by two policemen and placed in a dazed condition and a deserted spot opposite the National Gallery.

It was while he was standing there, encircled by, pigeons and forgotten by his fellow man, that there came to him a spiritual revelation. "Strange!" he thought; "I notice a certain inconsistency in myself, and even in my utterances. I am two men, one of whom is me and one not me; and the one which is not me is the one which causes me to fall into the arms of policemen and other troubles. The one which is me loves these pigeons, and desires to live quietly with my dog, not considering public affairs, which, indeed, seem to be suited to persons of another sort. Whence, then, comes the one which is not me? Can it be that it is derived from the sayings and writings of others, and is but a spurious spirit only meet to be outcast? Do I, to speak in the vernacular, care any buttons whether we stick to Gibraltar or not so long as men do but live in kindness? And if that is so, have I the right to say I do? Ought I not, rather, to be true to my private self and leave the course of public affairs to those who have louder voices and no private selves?" The thought was extremely painful, for it seemed to disclose to him grave inconsistency in the recent management of his life. And, thoroughly mortified, he turned round with a view of entering the National Gallery and soothing his spirit with art, when he was arrested by the placard which covered it announcing which town had taken which sum of bonds. This lighted up such a new vista of public utility that his brain would certainly have caught fire again if one of the policemen who had conducted him across the Square had not touched him on the arm, and said:

"How are you now, sir?"

"I am pretty well, thank you, policeman," replied Mr. Lavender, "and sorry that I occasioned so much disturbance."

"Don't mention it, sir," answered the policeman; "you came a nasty crump."

"Tell me," said Mr. Lavender, suddenly looking up into his face, "do you consider that a man is justified in living a private life? For, as regards my future, it is largely on your opinion that I shall act."

The policeman, whose solid face showed traces of astonishment, answered slowly: "As a general thing, a man's private life don't bear lookin' into, as you know, sir."

"I have not lived one for some time," said Mr. Lavender.

"Well," remarked the policeman, "if you take my advice you won't try it a-gain. I should say you 'adn't the constitution."

"I fear you do not catch my meaning," returned Mr. Lavender, whose whole body was aching from his fall; "it is my public life which tries me."

"Well, then, I should chuck it," said the policeman.

"Really?" murmured Mr. Lavender eagerly, "would you?"

"Why not?" said the policeman.

So excited was Mr. Lavender by this independent confirmation of his sudden longing that he took out half a crown.

"You will oblige me greatly," he said, "by accepting this as a token of my gratitude."

"Well, sir, I'll humour you," answered the policeman; "though it was no trouble, I'm sure; you're as light as a feather. Goin' anywhere in particular?" he added.

"Yes," said Mr. Lavender, rather faintly, "the Tube Station."

"Come along with me, then."

Mr. Lavender went along, not sorry to have the protection of that stalwart form, for his nerve was shaken, not so much by physical suffering as by the revelation he had received.

"If you'll take my tip, sir," said the policeman, parting from him, "you won't try no private life again; you don't look strong."

"Thank you, policeman," said Mr. Lavender musingly; "it is kind of you to take an interest in me. Good-bye!"

Safely seated in the Tube for Hampstead he continued the painful struggle of his meditations. "If, indeed," he thought, "as a public man I do more harm than good, I am prepared to sacrifice all for my country's sake and retire into private life. But the policeman said that would be dangerous for me. What, then, is left? To live neither a public nor a private life!"

This thought, at once painful and heroic, began to take such hold of him that he arrived at his house in a high fever of the brain.

XXI

AND ASCENDS TO PARADISE

Now when Mr. Lavender once slept over an idea it became so strong that no power on earth could prevent his putting it into execution, and all night long he kept Blink awake by tramping up and down his bedroom and planning the details of such a retirement as would meet his unfortunate case. For at once he perceived that to retire from both his lives without making the whole world know of it would be tantamount to not retiring. "Only by a public act," he thought, "of so striking a character that nobody can miss it can I bring the moral home to all public and private men." And a hundred schemes swarmed like ants in his brain. Nor was it till the cock crew that one adequate to this final occasion occurred to him.

"It will want very careful handling," he thought, "for otherwise I shall be prevented, and perhaps even arrested in the middle, which will be both painful and ridiculous. So sublime, however, was his idea that he shed many tears over it, and often paused in his tramping to regard the unconscious Blink with streaming eyes. All the next day he went about the house and heath taking a last look at objects which had been dear, and at mealtimes ate and drank even less than usual, absorbed by the pathos of his coming renunciation. He determined to make his preparations for the final act during the night, when Mrs. Petty would be prevented by Joe's snoring from hearing the necessary sounds; and at supper he undertook the delicate and harrowing task of saying good-bye to, his devoted housekeeper without letting her know that he, was doing it.

"Mrs - Petty," he said, trifling with a morsel of cheese, "it is useless to disguise, from you that I may be going a journey, and I feel that I shall not be able to part from all the care you have, bestowed on me without recording in words my heartfelt appreciation of your devotion. I shall miss it, I shall miss it terribly, if, that is, I am permitted to miss anything."

Mrs. Petty, whose mind instantly ran to his bed socks, answered: "Don't you worry, sir; I won't forget them. But wherever are you going now?"

"Ah!" said Mr. Lavender subtly, "it is all in the air at present; but now that the lime-trees are beginning to smell a certain restlessness is upon me, and you may see some change in my proceedings. Whatever happens to me, however, I commit my dear Blink to your care; feed her as if she were myself, and love her as if she were Joe, for it is largely on food and affection that dogs depend for happiness.

"Why, good gracious, sir," said Mrs. Petty, "you talk as if you were going for a month of Sundays. Are you thinking of Eastbourne?"

Mr. Lavender sighed deeply at that word, for the memory of a town where he had spent many happy days added to the gentle melancholy of his feelings on this last evening.

"As regards that I shall not inform you at present; for, indeed, I am by no means certain what my destination will be. Largely speaking, no pub - public man," he stammered, doubtful whether he was any longer that, "knows where he will be going to-morrow. Sufficient unto the day are the intentions in his head.

"Well, sir," said Mrs. Petty frankly, "you can't go anywhere without Joe or me, that's flat."

Mr. Lavender smiled.

"Dear Mrs. Petty," he murmured, "there are sacrifices one cannot demand even of the most faithful friends. But," he went on with calculated playfulness, "we need not consider that point until the day after to-morrow at least, for I have much to do in the meantime."

Reassured by those words and the knowledge that Mr. Lavender's plans seldom remained the same for more than two days, Mrs. Petty tossed her head slightly and went to the door. "Well, it is a mystery, I'm sure," she said.

"I should like to see Joe," said Mr. Lavender, with a lingering look at his devoted housekeeper.

"The beauty!" muttered Mrs. Petty; "I'll send him," and withdrew.

Giving the morsel of cheese to Blink, who, indeed, had eaten practically the whole of this last meal, Mr. Lavender took the moon-cat on his shoulder, and abandoned himself for a moment to the caresses of his two favourites.

"Blink," he said in a voice which trembled slightly, "be good to this moon-cat while I am away; and if I am longer than you expect, darling, do not be unhappy. Perhaps some day you will rejoin me; and even if we are not destined to meet again, I would not, in the fashion of cruel men, wish to hinder your second marriage, or to stand in the way of your happy forgetfulness of me. Be as light-hearted as you can, my dear, and wear no mourning for your master."

So saying, he flung his arms round her, and embraced her warmly, inhaling with the most poignant emotion her sheep-like odour. He was still engaged with her when the door was opened, and Joe came in.

"Joe," said Mr. Lavender resolutely, "sit down and light your pipe. You will find a bottle of pre-war port in the sideboard. Open it, and, drink my health; indeed, I myself will drink it too, for it may give me courage. We have been good friends, Joe," he went on while Joe was drawing the cork," and have participated in pleasant and sharp adventures. I have called you in at this moment, which may some day seem to you rather solemn, partly to shake your hand and partly to resume the discussion on public men which we held some days ago, if you remember."

"Ah!" said Joe, with his habitual insouciance, "when I told you that they give me the 'ump."

"Yes, what abaht it, sir? 'Ave they been sayin' anything particular vicious?" His face flying up just then with the cork which he was extracting encountered the expression on Mr. Lavender's visage, and he added:

"Don't take wot I say to 'eart, sir; try as you like you'll never be a public man."

Those words, which seemed to Mr. Lavender to seal his doom, caused a faint pink flush to invade his cheeks.

"No," continued Joe, pouring out the wine; you 'aven't got the brass in times like these. I dare say you've noticed, sir, that the times is favourable for bringing out the spots on the body politic. 'Ere's 'ealth!"

"Joe," said Mr. Lavender, raising the glass to his lips with solemnity, "I wish you a most happy and prosperous life. Let us drink to all those qualities which make you par excellence one of that great race, the best hearted in the world, which never thinks of tomorrow, never knows when it is beaten, and seldom loses its sense of humour.

"Ah!" returned Joe enigmatically, half-closing one of his greenish eyes, and laying the glass to one side of his reddish nose. Then, with a quick movement, he swallowed its contents and refilled it before Mr. Lavender had succeeded in absorbing more than a drop.

"I don't say," he continued, "but what there's a class o' public man that's got its uses, like the little 'un that keeps us all alive, or the perfect English gentleman what did his job, and told nobody nothin' abaht it. You can 'ave confidence in a man like that - - that's why 'e's gone an' retired; 'e's civilized, you see, the finished article; but all this raw material, this 'get-on' or 'get-out' lot, that's come from 'oo knows where, well, I wish they'd stayed there with their tell-you-how-to-do-it and their 'ymns of 'ate."

"Joe," said Mr. Lavender, "are you certain that therein does not speak the snob inherent in the national bosom? Are you not unconsciously paying deference to the word gentleman?"

"Why not, sir?" replied Joe, tossing off his second glass. "It'd be a fine thing for the country if we was all gentlemen - straight, an' a little bit stupid, and 'ad 'alf a thought for others." And he refilled his master's glass. "I don't measure a gentleman by 'is money, or 'is title, not even by 'is clothes - I measure 'im by whether he can stand 'avin' power in 'is 'ands without gettin' unscrupled or swollen 'eaded, an' whether 'e can do what he thinks right without payin' attention, to clamour. But, mind you, 'e's got to 'ave right thoughts too, and a feelin' 'eart. 'Ere's luck, sir."

Mr. Lavender, who, absorbed in his chauffeur's sentiments, had now drunk two glasses, rose from his, chair, and clutching his hair said: "I will not conceal from you, Joe, that I have always assumed every public man came up to that standard, at least."

"Crikey said Joe. 'Ave you really, sir? My Gawd! Got any use for the rest of this bottle?"

"No, Joe, no. I shall never have use for a bottle again."

"In that case I might as well," said Joe, pouring what remained into a tumbler and drinking it off. "Is there any other topic you'd like to mention? If I can 'ave any influence on you, I shall be very glad."

"Thank you, Joe," returned Mr. Lavender, "what I have

most need of at this moment is solitude and your good wishes. And will you kindly take Blink away, and when she has had her run, place her in my bedroom, with the window closed. Good-night, Joe. Call me late tomorrow morning.

"Certainly, sir. Good-night, sir."

"Good-night, Joe. Shake hands."

When Joe was gone, accompanied by the unwilling Blink, turning her beautiful dark eyes back to the last, Mr. Lavender sat down at his bureau, and drawing a sheet of paper to him, wrote at the top of it.

"My last Will and Testament."

It was a long time before he got further, and then entirely omitted to leave anything in it, completely preoccupied by the preamble, which gradually ran as follows:

"I, John Lavender, make known to all men by these presents that the act which I contemplate is symbolical, and must in no sense be taken as implying either weariness of life or that surrender to misfortune which is unbecoming to an English public gentleman." (Over this description of himself Mr. Lavender was obliged to pause some time hovering between the two designations, and finally combining them as the only way out of his difficulty.) "Long and painful experience has convinced me that only by retiring from the former can I retain the latter character, and only by retiring from both can I point the moral ever demanded by my countrymen. Conscious, indeed, that a mere act of private resignation would have no significance to the body politic, nor any deflecting influence on the national life, I have chosen rather to disappear in blue flame, so that every Englishman may take to heart my lesson, and learn from my strange fate how to be himself uninfluenced by the verbiage of others. At the same time, with the utmost generosity, I wish to acknowledge in full my debt towards all those great writers and speakers on the war who have exercised so intoxicating an influence on my mind." (Here followed an alphabetical list of names beginning with B and ending with S.)

"I wish to be dissociated firmly from the views of my chauffeur Joe Petty, and to go to my last account with an emphatic assertion that my failure to become a perfect public gentleman is due to private idiosync-rasies rather than to any conviction that it is impossible, or to anything but admiration of the great men I have mentioned. If anybody should wish to paint me after I am dead, I desire that I may he represented with my face turned towards the Dawn; for it is at that moment so symptomatic of a deep adoration - which I would scorn to make the common property of gossiping tongues - that I intend to depart. If there should be anything left of me - which is less than probable considering the inflammatory character of the material I design for my pyre - I would be obliged if, without giving anybody any trouble, it could be buried in my garden, with the usual Hampstead tablet.

"'JOHN LAVENDER, THE PUBLIC MAN, WHO DIED FOR HIS COUNTRY'S GOOD, LIVED HERE.'

"In conclusion, I would say a word to that land I have loved and served: 'Be not extreme! Distrust the words, of others. To yourself be true! As you are strong be gentle, as you are brave be modest! Beloved country, farewell!'"

Having written that final sentence he struggled long with himself before he could lay down the pen. But by this time the port he had drunk had begun to have its usual effect, and he fell into a doze, from which he was awakened five hours later by the beams of a full moon striking in on him.

"The hour has come," he thought, and, opening the French-window, he went out on to the lawn, where the dew lay white. The freshness in the air, the glamour of the moonlight, and the fumes of the port combined to make him feel strangely rhumantic, and if he had possessed a musical instrument he would very likely have begun to play on it. He spent some moments tracking to and fro in the dew before he settled on the centre of the lawn as the most suitable spot for the act which he contemplated, for thence he would be able to turn his last looks towards Aurora's bedroom-window without interference from foliage. Having drawn a twelve-foot circle in the dew with his toe he proceeded in the bright moonlight to the necessary accumulation of his funeral pile, conveying from his study, book by book, journal by journal, pamphlet by pamphlet, the hoarded treasures of the last four years; and as he carefully placed each one, building up at once a firm and cunning structure, he gave a little groan, thinking of the intoxications of the past, and all the glorious thoughts embodied in that literature. Underneath, in the heart of the pile, he reserved a space for the most inflammable material, which he selected from a special file of a special journal, and round the circumference of the lofty and tapering mound he carefully deposited the two hundred and four war numbers of a certain weekly, so that a ring of flame might lick well up the sides and permeate the more solid matter on which he would be sitting. For two hours he worked in the waning moonlight till he had completed this weird and heroic erection; and just before the dawn, sat down by the light of the candle with which he meant to apply the finishing touch, to compose that interview with himself whereby he intended to convey to the world the message of his act.

"I found him," he began, in the words of the interviewer, "sitting upon a journalistic pile of lovely leaves of thought, which in the dawning of a new day glowed with a certain restrained flamboyance, as though the passion stored within those exotic pages gave itself willingly to the 'eclaircissement' of the situation, and of his lineaments on which suffering had already set their stamp.

"'I should like you,' I said, approaching as near as I could, for the sparks, like little fireflies on a Riviera evening, were playing profoundly round my trousers, 'I should like to hear from your own lips the reasons which have caused you to resign.'

"'Certainly,' he replied, with the courtesy which I have always found characteristic of him in moments which would try the suavity of more ordinary men; and with the utmost calm and clarity he began to tell me the inner workings of his mind, while the growing dawn-light irradiated his wasted and expressive features, and the flames slowly roasted his left boot.

"'Yes,' he said quietly, and his eyes turned inwards, 'I have at last seen the problem clearly, and seen it whole. It is largely because of this that I have elected to seek the seclusion of another world. What that world contains for me I know not, though so many public men have tried to tell me; but it has never been my way to recoil from the Unknown, and I am ready for my journey beyond the wide world's end.'

"I was greatly struck by the large-hearted way in which he spoke those words, and I interrupted him to ask whether he did not think that there was something fundamental in the British character which would leap as one man at such an act of daring sacrifice and great adventure.

"'As regards that,' he replied fearlessly, while in the light of the ever-brightening dawn I could, see the suspender on his right leg gradually charring, so that he must already have been in great pain, 'as regards that, it is largely the proneness of the modern British to leap to verbal extremity which is inducing me to afford them this object-lesson in restraint and commonsense. Ouch !'

"This momentary ejaculation seemed to escape him in spite of all his iron control; and the smell of burning flesh brought home to me as nothing else, perhaps, could have done the tortures he must have been suffering.

"'I feel,' he went on very gravely, 'that extravagance of word and conduct is fatal to my country, and having so profoundly experienced its effects upon myself, I am now endeavouring by a shining example to supply a remedy for a disease which is corroding the vitals and impairing the sanity of my countrymen and making them a race of second-hand spiritual drunkards. Ouch!'

"I confess that at this moment the tears started to my eyes, for a more sublime show than the spectacle of this devoted man slowly roasting himself to death before my eyes for the good of his country I had seldom seen. It had a strange, an appalling interest, and for nothing on earth could I have torn my gaze away. I now realized to the full for the first time the will-power and heroism of the human species, and I rejoiced with a glorious new feeling that I was of the same breed as this man, made of such stern stuff that not even a tear rolled down his cheeks to quench the flames that leaped around him ever higher and higher. And the dawn came up in the eastern sky; and I knew that a great day was preparing for mankind; and with my eyes fixed upon him as he turned blacker and blacker I let my heart loose in a great thanksgiving that I had lived to see this moment. It was then that he cried out in a loud voice:

"'I call Aurora to witness that I have died without a falter, grasping a burning spear, to tilt at the malpractice which has sent me mad!' And I saw that he held in his fast-consuming hand a long roll of journals sharpened to a point of burning flame.

"'Aurora!' he cried again, and with that enigmatic word on his lips was incinerated in the vast and towering belch of the devouring element.

"It was among the most inspiring sights I have ever witnessed."

When Mr. Lavender had completed that record, whose actuality and wealth of moving detail had greatly affected him, and marked it "For the Press-Immediate," he felt very cold. It was, in fact, that hour of dawn when a shiver goes through the world; and, almost with pleasurable anticipation he took up his lighted candle and stole shivering out to his pile, rising ghostly to the height of some five feet in the middle of the dim lawn whereon a faint green tinge was coming with the return of daylight. Having reached it, he walked round it twice, and readjusted four volumes of the history of the war as stepping-stones to the top; then lowering the candle, whose flame burned steadily in the stillness, he knelt down in the grey dew and set fire to an article in a Sunday paper. Then, sighing deeply, he returned to his little ladder and, with some difficulty preserving his balance, mounted to the top, and sat down with his legs towards the house and his eyes fixed on Aurora's bedroom-window. He had been there perhaps ten minutes before he realized that nothing was happening below him, and, climbing down again, proceeded to the aperture where he had inserted the burning print. There, by the now considerable daylight, he saw that the flame had gone out at the words "The Stage is now set for the last act of this colossal world drama." And convinced that Providence had intended that heartening sentence to revive his somewhat drooping courage, he thought, "I, too, shall be making history this morning," and relighting the journal, went on his hands and knees and began manfully to blow the flames. . . . . .

Now the young lady in the adjoining castle, who had

got out of bed, happened, as she sometimes did, to go to the window for a look at the sun rising over Parliament Hill. Attracted by the smell of burning paper she saw Mr. Lavender in this act of blowing up the flames.

"What on earth is the poor dear doing now?" she thought. "This is really the limit!" And slipping on her slippers and blue dressing-gown she ensconced herself behind the curtain to await developments.

Mr. Lavender had now backed away from the flames at which he had been blowing, and remained on his hands and knees, apparently assuring himself that they had really obtained hold. He then rose, and to her intense surprise began climbing up on to the pile. She watched him at first with an amused astonishment, so ludicrous was his light little figure, crowned by stivered-up white hair, and the expression of eager melancholy on his thin, high-cheekboned face upturned towards her window. Then, to her dismay, she saw that the flame had really caught, and, suddenly persuaded that he had some crazy intention of injuring himself with the view, perhaps, of attracting her attention, she ran out of her room and down the stairs, and emerging from the back door just as she was, circled her garden, so that she might enter Mr. Lavender's garden from behind him, ready for any eventuality. She arrived within arm's reach of him without his having heard her, for Blink, whose anxious face as she watched her master wasting, could be discerned at the bedroom-window, was whining, and Mr. Lavender himself had now broken into a strange and lamentable chantey, which, in combination with the creeping flutter of the flames in the weekly journals encircling the base of the funeral pyre, well-nigh made her blood curdle.

"Aurora," sang Mr. Lavender, in that most dolorous voice,

> "Aurora, my heart I bring,
> For I know well it will not burn,
> Oh! when the leaves puff out in Spring
> And when the leaves in Autumn turn
> Think, think of me!
> Aurora, I pass away!
> Upon my horse of air I ride;
> Here let my grizzled ashes stay,
> But take, ah! take my heart inside!
> Aurora! Aurora!"

At this moment, just as a fit of the most uncontrollable laughter was about to seize her, she saw a flame which had just consumed the word Horatio reach Mr. Lavender's right calf.

"Oh!" he cried out in desperate tones, stretching up his arms to the sky. "Now is my hour come! Sweet-sky, open and let me see her face! Behold! behold her with the eyes of faith. It is enough. Courage, brother; let me now consume in silence!" So saying, he folded his arm tightly across his breast and closed his lips. The flame rising to the bottom of the weekly which had indeed been upside down, here nipped him vigorously, so that with a wholly unconscious movement he threw up his little legs, and, losing his balance, fell backwards into the arms of Aurora, watchfully outstretched to receive him. Uplifted there, close to that soft blue bosom away from the reek of the flame, he conceived that he was consumed and had passed already from his night of ghosts and shadows into the arms of the morning, and through his swooning lips came forth the words:

"I am in Paradise."

www.ingramcontent.com/pod-product-compliance
Lightning Source LLC
Chambersburg PA
CBHW031640040426
42453CB00006B/165